Daily Reflections 2002

An Anthology of Poetry

First published in Great Britain in 2002 by
TRIUMPH HOUSE
Remus House,
Coltsfoot Drive,
Peterborough, PE2 9JX
Telephone (01733) 898102

HB ISBN 1 90422 030 4
SB ISBN 1 90422 031 2

Contents

The Poems

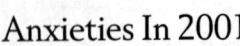

Anxieties In 2001

Will it be peace, or will it be war
And whatever will it be for?
Planes will fly high up in the sky
And down below many people will die.

They'll all claim to have God on their side
But actually it won't be for Him to decide.
So let's hope the world doesn't go mad
For poor suffering humanity it's ever so sad!

Henry Rayner

Smiles

Today I'll smile and be happy
Whatever befalls
If I get put down, I'll not frown
I'll keep on smiling
I'll give to one who insults me
An answering smile
If smiles are as infectious
As I think they are
There could be an epidemic
Spreading near and far.

Dora Watkins

17

The Sky

When the night is dark and you can't see afar
Surely if you look you will see a star
The sky is full of wonder from morning till night
Dawn brings its beauty at the first light
Sunlight by daytime, twilight the moon
Because of these wonders tempt crooners to croon
Have you stared at a rainbow, kept staring in awe
One still finds magnificence even seen before
The clouds with their puffiness move slowly on high
Something of beauty is the lovely blue sky
An artist can't match all the colours up there
Our Lord made them all for us to share

Brownie

Loving Each Other

We shouldn't fall out
Over different religions
Everyone has the right
To make decisions
I'm sure God above
Wouldn't judge only care
For to follow your faith
Is your right anywhere
Loving each other's
The right thing to do
Not making war
As others may do
It doesn't solve problems
Just causes more strife
Then hurt and anguish
To blight people's lives
Be tolerant of others
See their point of view
And follow your faith
Is all God asks of you

Jeanette Gaffney

19

Thank You

I know that I have confidence,
I know if I'm not heard, I can shout,
I know I can master anything,
I know that without a doubt.

I know the world's my oyster,
I know I'm as good as the rest,
I know no one's above me,
And I might even be the best.

You gave me all this confidence,
You said hold your head high,
You gave me the strength I needed,
When all I could do was cry.

For all these things you've given me,
For giving my outlook a clearer view,
I'll repay you one day my love,
But in the meantime I want to thank you.

Anne Leeson

Friendship

Friendship means so many things
As we go through the years
A shoulder there to cry on
Someone to dry our tears
Laughter shared when someone cares
And though our ways may part
There will always be a corner
Where you stay in my heart
Out of sight - not out of mind
Though the days go by so fast
Memories are always there
We don't forget the past
Love can have no boundaries
Thoughts cannot be chained
They can travel o'er the miles
Until we meet again.

Lydia Barnett

Thinking . . .

My thinking is not sure enough
I must improve each thought.
Else all the battle plans I've made
I'll either fail or I'll abort.
So what if I have dark, dark clouds
optimism rides the storm.
'Til I find the silver lining
and then a rainbow, warm.
Step from the clouds has become my thought,
'tis one I shall let grow.
Until the cloud is far behind
and the rainbow is on show.
I'm building up the optimist,
the negative must fade.
I know so much of rainbows
and prefer them to the shade.
                    Of course!

Rosie Hues

It's Free

Families, brothers and sisters,
Husbands, children and wives,
All contribute in their own way
To help us achieve fuller lives.
Mothers and fathers are different.
They rear us and show us the way,
They give all their love to sustain us,
Never once asking for pay.

Rodney Epstein

Beautiful Words

We must never think we're on our own,
There are surprises on the way,
People stop you in your tracks
When they have beautiful words to say.

People should never be afraid
To encourage or to praise,
As it's these little words of encouragement
That help us alter our ways.

They help us stand taller, more erect,
More able to face the world
With a confidence that's not 'put on'
As problems at us are hurled.

It's lovely to know that people care
That they think you are of some worth,
That perhaps there is a reason
For us being here on earth.

How much does it cost to say
'Well done' or 'I'm proud of you'
How much does it cost to say
'You know what you should do'

How much does it cost to say
'You did a good job today'
And how much does it cost to say
'I thought of you today'

If people only realised
What a difference it can make
When someone, not only thinks things,
But takes the trouble to speak.

Hilary Vint

24

Time Out

If you're feeling far too busy
And you're really in a spin,
If your head is getting dizzy
And your patience growing thin;
Take a breath, make time to pause,
Let yourself be calm;
For if you stop, it will not cause
The world to come to harm.

Charlotte Dudley

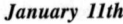

Trust

Trust is a word
A feeling we are given
Trust is earned
It is deserved
Broken trust is never forgiven

We can forget
We can put it in the past
Shut it in a corner of our mind
Close our eyes to its repetition
But how long will that last?

Carey Sellwood

Onward Together

Onward together dear friends we must go,
For once we have lost the track.
It's never so good to look back,
For remember, life will never bring us again,
Chances that have swept away.
Keep a dream in your heart,
For another bright new day.
We must look forward to some happy times,
That's waiting near our way.
There is always hope for sunshine,
To follow a happy heart,
Long before we all have to part.

Elisabeth Dill Perrin

27

This Day

Hold in your hands this day,
It is a thing most precious
For you alone to mould, to savour,
Yours alone.

Our lives span many days,
Each one unique and precious,
Never to come again.

Do not squander the hours
That God has given us.
Let each one be as a shining jewel
Set in a circle of gold.

Past days hold memories
Both sad and joyous,
Times that we regret.
We know not what the future holds,
How many days are still to come,
So live each minute to the full,
Let joy be in your heart
And let it spread to others, too.

Share these glad moments
And rich will be reward.
Let there be no regrets,
This day comes only once to us.

Roma Davies

The Tide Of Life

Life is like the sea
Sometimes it swells
The heart is full of joy
The full of sadness
The sea's tides ebb away
Then come back full of life
Like the heart bursting with love and laughter
Then breaking with unhappiness
Life is a journey
Up and down like the rolling waves
Move with the tides
On sadness do not dwell
For tomorrow may bring a tide that swells

Gertrude Schöen

Peace

Peace is not born amid promises
and good intentions, nor is it the offspring
of violence and aggression. It is the child
of tolerance and understanding.
Peace will not grow from endless talk and
bartering - it thrives on the hand of friendship
and guidance touched with gentleness
and dedication.
Peace does not learn to walk alone -
it needs companions to share
the stony path and shoulder the heavy load.
Peace lives among hearts that are true,
that care and love for each other,
not in an atmosphere of hate, greed and envy.
Peace dies from neglect, from abuse
and ignorance - yet deep within us all
is the strength and the courage
to keep peace alive forever.

Donald S Ferguson

Life's Journey

The journey through life is not an easy road
and lessons are often learnt upon the way
Maybe the road ahead was blocked
but somehow a way round was created
and when you become lost and confused
the path home was discovered
so no matter how difficult or impossible
the way ahead may seem
any obstacle set in your path will be overcome
for all that is needed
is the belief and faith to find yourself

Jan Maissen

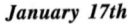

The Beautitudes

(Matthew 5:3-12) are:

Blessed are the poor in spirit, for theirs is the kingdom of Heaven.

Blessed are those who mourn, for they shall be comforted.

Blessed are the meek, for they shall inherit the earth.

Blessed are those who hunger and thirst for righteousness, for they shall be satisfied.

Blessed are the merciful, for they shall obtain mercy.

Blessed are the pure in heart, for they shall see God.

Blessed are the peacemakers, for they shall be called sons of God.

Blessed are those who are persecuted for righteousness' sake, for theirs is the kingdom of Heaven.

Blessed are you when men revile you and persecute you and utter all kinds of evil against you falsely on My account. Rejoice and be glad, for your reward is great in Heaven.

Take Heed In What You Do

Take heed in what you say, and do
Albeit, to some - the opportunities few
For that man, woman or child you just passed by
Without acknowledging may have lost you a friend one day

Take heed in what you do, and say
Aside from time spent at work
You must set aside time to play and pray
No matter how long or cluttered the day
Be sure to try and find a way

Time travels like an express train
Station stops like on life's journey can be few
Wells for drinking and times of spiritual thirst differing as to one's journey
Offering to lend a helping hand can be rewarding
If not, instantly, tomorrow or another day
Your journey too may become bumpy one day
Your bed lumpy, for hidden dangers await those who los their way

Take heed in what you do, or say
A light may be on in your window, today
But, tomorrow a blanket of darkness might shroud your world
Before, that is, you found time to offer some help or pray

A problem shared is a problem halved, so they say
Politicians have told us all to clean up our acts
But I ask you, no matter how good they might talk
Has other than our own hard work got the job done
Dug a ditch or mended fences in need of repair

Your deeds are watched over by God every minute of the day
Watching from above, behind one's shoulder or yonder's grass covered boulder

So, take heed in what you do and say whether you be young or old
Straight or gay, for together we all can make this world a better place to stay

Maurice Hope

33

A Psalm of David

The Holy Bible: King James Version 2000 Psalm 23

1. The *Lord* is my shepherd; I shall not want.

2. He maketh me to lie down in green pastures:
he leadeth me beside the still waters. Rev. 7.17

3. He restoreth my soul:
he leadeth me in the paths of righteousness for his name's sake.

4. Yea, though I walk through the valley of the shadow death,
I will fear no evil: for thou art with me;
thy rod and thy staff they comfort me.

5. Thou preparest a table before me in the presence of mine enemies:
thou anointest my head with oil;
my cup runneth over.

6. Surely goodness and mercy shall follow me all the days of my life:
and I will dwell in the house of the *Lord* for ever.

Let It Be

Let it be
That on tender feet
You come to me
With a quickening heavy heart
And sorrow in your darkened eyes

Let it be
When all my joy be gone
You come to me
And betrayal all be yours

Let it be
You could pass this way
With many years gone through
And still you come to me

But are we not the same?
Of blood and bone
So many words you spare me not
Let it be of hurt and blame

Moira Clelland

Grandson

He came as prelude to the dawn
Amid a raging thunderstorm
The thunder was Gabriel's Horn
Announcing baby boy was born
To Emma his sister sibling
'Elvis' has entered the building!

John Smurthwaite

Civilisation

Civilisation, look what it's done for us, it's brought us near the end,
Manmade power he also made you and I, what went wrong my friend?

Evolution, look where it's brought us, they say we came from apes,
And through the years we've fought war after war and now there's
no escape.

Modern technology has replaced nature, it's a wonder what progress
can do,
 And computers have taken over the minds of me and you.

Sticks and stones were what we fought with and now they've turned
to bombs,
Blowing people up we don't even know, only the place they come from.

Civilisation look what it's done for us, we don't know who we are.
And looking back on our existence, I think we've gone too far.

Evolution, look where it's brought us, it's brought us near the end,
And one day the button will be pressed and what will happen then?

The human race will be finished, no one to carry it one,
No more violence and no more wars because man has gone.

Paul Athorne

O Lord I Pray

Each night I lay down on my bed,
My prayers I say inside my head,
I thank the Lord for all he's done,
When times were hard and not much fun.

For my family Lord, I ask please care,
The love you have with them please share,
Protect them as they pass through life,
Dear Lord look down upon my wife.

Our dear grandchildren Lord I pray,
Please tend for them by night and day,
Give them health to cope with life,
Please help them free from fear and strife.

When judgement day is drawing near,
Please fill our hearts with joy not fear,
Forgive our earthly sins I pray,
Before from this world we pass away.

G D Eccleston

My Prayer

I fold my hands and pray to Thee
Each night within my bed -
It is a time that I hold dear
When thanks, and needs are said.

I thank Thee first for loving care
To me, and those I love.
I put my trust in Thee, dear Lord,
Watching o'er us from above.

I ask that you do heal the sick,
Help those in times of need.
Look kindly on the poor, distressed,
And where there's starving, feed.

I ask of Thee to stem the pain
Of those recently bereaved,
And thank Thee for the blessings
By all mankind, received.

I thank Thee just for being there
To help when things look bleak –
I know that you will comfort me
When with you each night I speak.

Joyce Hockley

Reflections On A Shattered Mirror

Ever since you came,
Reasons have stood still.
And your stupid game
Has left me feeling ill.
Nightly you would tease
With your ghostly eyes.
You only displease
And choke me on your lies.
I don't know your name
I don't know you at all.
It seems like you're lame.
From which cloud did you fall?
I have seen your face before,
But I can't remember where!
I am never sure.
Oh, all you do is stare!
And I don't want to see your face.
And I don't want to hear your voice.
No, I don't want to see your face,
But I haven't got a choice!
Oh, you seem so still and dead,
But your tears won't ever show.
I have choked on every word you said,
And now wish that you would go.
Please, please go away.
Don't ever come again.
Go away, away, away.
Don't ever call again.
I am the mirror,
And you - the reflected.
You are an error
That was never corrected.

Oh, you broke me.
The image is now dead.
Oh, how you hurt me.
My heart has truly bled.
Fragments lay in shame
Upon the dirty floor.
I am now an empty frame,
Not like I was before!
Now I am in pieces,
Do you feel good?
The pain never seizes.
You can't be understood.
Through my broken eyes
I can see you scream,
And cry all your lies.
It is a real dream.
Now you are still,
Dead upon the floor.
Your eyes don't look ill.
Truth has won the war.,
The girl you unlawfully had
Told her father, you know.
He took it so bad
And your blood had to flow.
She was a virgin
And you stole her heart.
Her father heard of the sin
And blew your head apart!
I am the mirror
I lay broken in shame.
Just like all mirrors . . .
We know your game!

Peter Steele

Life - Past, Present And Future

We do not remember
Our life before birth,
Our being before we awakened on Earth
Anymore than the deep sleep of last night
When our season took flight
And our awareness died,
To be conscious once more at first light.
We lived long ago in ancestral seed,
In ancestral beings, souls and spirits
Or we don't live now.
For without previously existing
How can we eternal, life inherit?
Today is the afterlife of yesterday,
Tomorrow the afterlife of today.
Can you see and hear
Every sight and sound of 10 o'clock, 1st of September, last year?
You were alive at the time
But your life then you've forgotten.
Can you remember the day you were born?
Or what you did on your birthday at the age of three?
It wouldn't do for the mind to be cluttered and torn
Between remembering the 'then' as opposed to the 'now' or what will be.
Could you have once lived as a dinosaur, crocodile, cow or apple tree?
What will be your form, what state will you be in,
A thousand millennia from now?
We reap as we have sown.
A mere half century ago we had holocausts, atomic bombs and war.
Is that what we reaped, and why we're now sowing
More violence, more bloodshed, what for?
If we don't learn from the past
We encourage, what's worse -
A future of meaningless manmade force.
If we conform with nature, the Earth's nature, man's nature, God's nature.

We could prepare for a far better future culture.
Why are we given a life to live
Without love and compassion and the need to forgive?
Make the most of what is, to fashion hereafter
A world of joy, happiness and bliss.
Let's not make ourselves any madder or dafter!
We can raise devils to their angelic prior status
And fill this Earth with mirth and laughter
If we only remember why we're here and who made us
God grant us breath of life to recreate and inflate us!

David W Hill

41

Life Is What You Make It

Do you know how it feels to feel right down
To hit rock bottom and to hit the ground?
It hits deep down inside you, stop caring or feeling
Like a ball of string within you, carries on reeling.
Your head is in shambles like a ski slope rambles,
It's like being on a gambling wheel with your mind in mangles.
You can't to see the light for the dark shadows of your mind
You try to search for reason and confidence is hard to find.
Don't give up, it's a natural feeling to fear and be unbeguiling
It happens to someone every minute you're not alone and I'm not lying.
You have to fight to be strong to build up your resistance.
Because if we all gave in my friend so easily, where is our existence?
It's the system that fails us, it could be one person's dream.
And the anxiety that follows drowns some of us in streams.
Don't give up on a dream, don't stop caring or sharing or disbelieving,
You're better than that, don't let your intelligence be insulted,
while you're still breathing.
You're here and alive, reach for the skies, be the voice that reaches out.
Let the dreamers know that you also have a voice that can scream and shout.
You've got to reach inside yourself for everything you have lost,
At the end of the day there's no one to blame and we all count the cost.
In a real world we all should get on but that was yesterday and that's already gone.
Waken up there's someone worse than you in this cruel world and that is true,
What gives you the right to be greedy, selfish, indulgent, just because you're you
When there is hunger, war, plight and plunder, pillage, death, rape,
murder and blunder,
You're not the only person on this Earth and that is a fact, it costs
nothing to love or hug someone and that is what is lacked.
So when you're feeling down and out just remember what life's really about.

Take the time to look around life is so precious as you will have found.
And if you exist take my advice or this my friend could be your last round,
Life is what you make it, it all depends on you,
So take it or break it or take my hand and let's shake it.

I Smith

42

Slumber

I am lying on a bed of ferns
Listening to the great god Pan
Playing reedy pipes in my ear;

I am lost to the world,
I wander through dreams
Under the walls of an Arran castle;

Through secret gardens, tended by Time
Alien trees, evergreen leaves, light sparkling
On water. I see a stone sundial;

I am asleep, I am awake, I am a dream.

John Doyle

The Office

The patter
of the chatter
youth-strewn,
yuppie-filled.
Moisturiser poised
on the ledge.

'Vogue' opened
intermittently
or frequently;
depending on the diligence.
Fax machine
purring,
telephone ringing,
voice mail buzzing.

The clang
of empty coffee
cups;
the fag breaks,
the hiccups,
the hassle
of the
working week.

The whiz.
The hum-drum.
The sordidness.

The nine
to
five.

Caroline Baker

We Teach It

Our thinking couldn't be more wrong,
If we want wars to cease,
No dialogue however long,
Could bring a lasting peace,
Most human conflict's based upon,
A deep mistrust or hate,
And they've been smouldering so long,
Wise counsel is too late,
And though we try the best we can,
For the peace that we desire,
It only takes one angry man,
To reignite the fire,
No matter how we mediate,
No peace will ever last,
While there are those who love to hate,
In memory of the past,
The cause is not a mystery,
We're monumental fools,
Most hatred stems from history,
We teach it in our schools.

Matthew L Burns

45

High As A Kite

High as a kite, think I'll have a little drink tonight,
because what happened today, was out of sight.
A few months ago, I wrote nine poems in one day,
and I wondered what it would be like, if ever,
I had nine poems published in one day.

This morning I found out, first the postman posted
four large, brown letters, pleasing me immediately.
Then he posted another five, through my letterbox,
and the feeling was one of joy, very intensely.

I danced around my living room,
playing my favourite music, loudly.
Full of hope for the future
shouting out, 'I'm a writer,' proudly.

What a way to start your morning!

And the very next day I had six short stories published!

Danny Coleman

Porch God

On the porch
in summer darkness
drops of rainy sadness fall.
In the lilac silence
God collects my prayers,
a summer porch God
only I can see.

Marion Schoeberlein

47

The Weakest Link

God won't vote me off His team
If I become the weakest link
In life's uncompromising chain,
And He won't criticise the way
I try to answer night and day
The questions causing me such pain.

He won't permanently vote
Against time when I'm incorrect
Or find it difficult to speak,
And He won't judge me constantly
Along the path of destiny
Or if my reasoning is weak.

God won't vote me off His team
Whenever I have failed to bank
My faith and trust within His care,
And He won't jeopardise my right
To answer freely and ignite
A consciousness in disrepair.

He won't vote incessantly
Against my insincerity
When questioning the simple truth,
And He won't reprimand my soul
Or denigrate its worldly role
That was determined in my youth.

God won't vote me off His team
If I have proved beyond all doubt
To be the weakest link in life,
And He won't coldly say *'Goodbye'*
When I have failed to answer why
My spirit's weaknesses are rife.

Iaian W Wade

Clouds

These clouds are not the same clouds that we used to watch
They have silver linings, as the old clouds did.
They chill us with the blocking out of light
and life
and hope.
I never noticed that before.
I watch alone. You watch alone,
wrapped in your growing shadow of despair.
Perhaps you do not see the silver lining
now that I am not there to point it out.
I see it. Gloom bejewelled,
tinsel vanity.

A F Brown

49

Sleepy Dust

'It's sleepy dust,' my mother used to say,
  As - drowsy eyelids over waking eyes -
With gentle finger she would brush away
  The tiny grit that over night - time dries.

And I would wake to feel her morning kiss;
  In these first moments neither doubt nor fear
From yesterday remained, and lacking this
  Another day's adventure started clear.

I wonder, can it be when we awake
  From that last sleep, if so indeed it be,
No pain or grief from mortal life we take -
  'It's sleepy dust,' as Mother said to me.

Kathleen M Hatton

Aura Of Chemainus - Canada

A stillness, a quiet, and yet, a depth of sound,
Beyond our comprehension.
A wooded glade so beautiful and light,
Conveying a mystical assurance of serenity,
And peace.
The street, where houses portrayed artistic simplicity,
And gardens held legends of wealth,
With their creations of colour.
Murals of historical value, displayed for appreciation
Of past times, captivated the imagination,
Beyond belief.
Skill of the workers, vibrated from the scenes,
Such was the intensity of dedication.
A dream with reality . . .

Lorna Tippett

On The Wind

When I am gone:
Look for me on the wind;
See my shape in the shadows under the trees;
Hear my crunching footfalls
On the gravel of the drive;
Watch for the dint of my shoes
On the wet green of the lawn;
Learn that I have
Joined the birds
In their shrubbery chorus,
Praising the spring,
That I am smiling
In the blossoming of the first rose.
Always I shall be there
Watching over you
When my tangible days are done.
How could it be otherwise
When it has been my duty
And delight to care for you
Down all those years?
How could the mere sloughing of my body
Change all that?
So, and especially,
Watch for me by moonlight.
I shall be there.
Always it was our time.

Ted Harriott

52

The Creek And Yachts (Noss Mayo)

They lie there eloquently
Like ghosts in the Autumn haze,
Lying at anchor beneath the squall,
They watch, as young children play.

Silently they yawn majestically there,
And we watch the swans dabbling,
Fishing under the water for minnows,
I could but only wonder, stop, and stare.

The still water laps at the bows,
Tilting there, from start to stern,
The tide retreating, as we continue to stare
At the mystical world we care to share.

The air cool, but warm in breath,
We watch the water breathe in and out,
As the sleepy village towers above the slopes,
Watching silently, with tender view.

Now we return to the warmth of a fire,
As we turn our way onwards, back to home,
Leaving this scene, softly given,
By a strange light, we travel forth.

Rosemary E Pearson

My Sweet Darling Child

(To Mary)

Here, lies my darling
not awake to see me cry,
my heart is aching for my
sweet darling child.
Seeing earth, cold and dry
let me cry.
The birds I see fly, then
pass your earthly home,
where my angel I can't take you home
I cannot linger in this place
where your body lies, your soul
has gone, to our loved ones in the
sky,
No more tears, or cares, I'll
let you go, to that heavenly
place, and you will see me
daily, thinking of you, my
sweet darling child. Paola.

Dori Lewis

The Beard

I am a beard
Chin coverer
Chin warmer
Briskly
Bum fluff
Disguise
Unshaven
Non shaven
Remington Shaver Rejecter
Bic rejecter
Food collector
Skin tickler
Face mask
Jeremy Beadle
Santa Claus
White
Grey, brown
Ginger, black
Short
Long
Billy goat
Many a man
Dislike a beard
I am a beard.

David J Hall

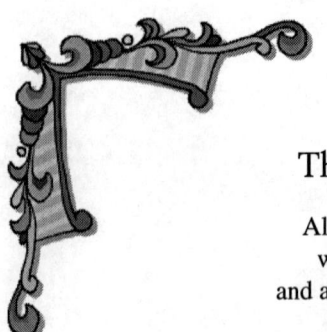

The Flotation Tank

All is silence in darkness
where I close my eyes
and am borne on saline waves
to mythical climes.

Now alone relaxed I smile,
gentler on myself,
subdued by the guardian angel
of fossilised shreds.

Biology mixed with myth,
nurturing life,
and the secluded waters warmth
assuaging my childish dreads.

While far above me,
the bright, vast constellations
are more than the grains of sand
scattered on earth.

But in the flotation tank
where I close my eyes,
the perimeters of touch -
extend beyond time.

Delia Marheineke

A Man

He's an old man now, and walks with a stick.
His hair is white and his eyes are dim
but I can remember when he was young
with a sprightly walk and full of fun.
He once was strong with a steady gait.
His eyes glistened and he seemed to wait.

He joked and laughed and understood.
His energy carried him - life was good
and nothing too hard for him to do.
The two of us managed to weather through.
Now he struggles bravely and has to be helped.
His life seems to be over but he does not yelp.

He can still see and walk a little,
like an angry bull, he is never still.
He tries to get started but the feeling soon fades.
He now has to fail to the end of his days,
but his courage is there, and he does not give up
He'll battle on - and he doesn't like fuss.

His children show him great affection
They'll do what they can and won't forget him,
His seeds were sown in better days
and others continue in their own ways.
Man waits alone and remembers the past,
that's all he can do because nothing lasts.

Doris E Pullen

57

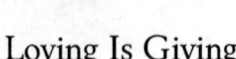

Loving Is Giving

Do you know the joy of love,
shining down from up above,
the warmth and security, I feel
in me, when I pray for God to set
me free,
my heart lifts my spirit shifts
to a place I'm so safe to be,
I know he's there especially for me
because I can see he's truly the key,
angels up above are helping me.
There comes a time when I have to greet
them, but if I think of God when I'm
all alone I know he will surely show
me the way home.
I'm to be a better person try to be good
just as the commandments say we should.

W Deaves

58

If Only . . .

If I were a puddle,
I wouldn't be deep.
Sharp, jagged, coarse stones
Would peer out from the surface
And wouldn't plunge at all.

If I were an insect,
I wouldn't be a butterfly.
Swirling, flashing, swan-like wings
Would fold beneath their casing
And wouldn't show at all.

If I were a bird,
I wouldn't be an eagle,
Soaring, flickering, lively eyes
Would stare within the head
And wouldn't look at all.

If I were an animal,
I wouldn't be a bat.
Pin-pricked, fleshy, open ears
Would close beneath the shutters
And wouldn't hear at all.

Jillian Shields

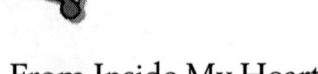

From Inside My Heart, To You

I awake as the sun rises, as the birds begin to sing.
I awake from a night of dreaming.

The water of the shower washes away the memories of the dreams
I had of you last night.
How I wish the night could last forever.

As I dress for work I wonder if I am in your thoughts?
You're constantly on my mind.

The day goes on and still the thought of you is heavy on my mind,
and pounding in my heart.
How I wish we could be together . . .
At sunrise, at sunset.
Walking, talking, laughing and holding each other closely.

You're always in my thoughts, in my dreams and deep inside my heart.
You hold the key.
You're the one that I want.

Until I met you I tried to keep my heart locked.
That way I'd never get hurt.
My dreams and most inner secrets were my own, until I shared them with you.
You taught me to open my heart and believe in myself and in my dreams.

You made me believe soul mates exist, and that love is the most powerful feeling a
person can feel.

You're the one I've been looking for since I heard the fairy tale story of Cinderella.
You're my Prince Charming and I want to be your Princess.

When I'm lying awake at night looking up at the star lit sky
I wonder if you're gazing up at the same bright star as I am.
One day I hope to make love to you under those very stars.

We agreed once that the best things in life are the 'not things'
The things we dream of, and the things we can only imagine with our hearts.

Well now I know that's not true . . .
For the best thing in my life and my heart is truly You!

Lynsey Tocker

Sweet Friendship Again

Up from the ashes, the phoenix
Dashes its foot against the past disaster,
The master redeeming
The teeming mass of hurt.

The fields become green!
A scene bathed in love appears
And sears time from eternity.
It's back again, sweet friendship!
Now carrying a deeper vein
In the skein of life.
More understanding, handing
Freedom to each.
See, a peach ripe for eating!

A new view, a freshness surges,
Urges a flower into bloom, for
The loom of the weaver
Is never still.

Sweet friendship again!
A glance, a chance to meet
And greet each other
In this moment.

Judith Thomas

For The Love That Is Meant To Be

How can I convey
I'll love you more upon the break of this
particular day?
Our destinies are entwined
criss crossing life's well trodden path?
Beside the crystal clear waters
that match the sparkle in your eyes
do I guess, do I choose?
Are you ready for what is about to come?
The whirlwind of change with the autumn tints
that are yet to come?
Come band with me upon a union of gold
may the frost in your heart slowly thaw
maybe not this year, maybe next hey?
Just let go of all that hate cast your fate upon
the calling beckoning that's so prevalent in the winds
of change
I feel it even more believe you me
this feeling is no longer strange to me!
Please, please open up to me
will you marry me?

Jonathan Covington

62

Meditation

It's all private and confidential,
Happiness is satisfaction,
Life has its discomforts,
But still it is all,
Private and confidential.

Between me and you,
There are but a few,
Inner peace, energy release,
Meditation,
Beneficial - calm,
Cure - heal,
What do you get,
Shear pleasure,
Tranquillity - peace,
Throughout life
I found the right way
There's only one way,
Meditation.

Amarjit Bhambra

Hear Yourself

An inner deepness of inner thought,
of inner body of that I was taught.
To focus of my eyes in time, for of the way you
have the light, of verse of song and flight.
To come to see of river of sight, to bath in the
waters and be cleansed tonight.
It can be beautiful the hope there, to inspire,
to break down not far from you.
A little thought that has a far, a tale in sight of
yester years or of that night.
A calling of a menu a menu of time of day,
but a calling of a word, of what more but I will say,
I will not give up, I will see it to that day.
Like a shell it is ready to break, but inside it can escape.
The body a shape of flesh inside, of all the body
parts, it can come outside.
In what I mean, it has been seen, it can give life
to other human beings.
Of water we need, from the sky to the ground,
it will feed the earth all around and see of how
easy it can be found.
To be trapped and locked away, inside and cannot tell.
Like a world of your own, because you can lock
yourself away in a room and never know.

Shauna Hamilton

The Dance

Dancing parcels of light, flashed across my eyes
as silhouetted castanets
clicked to the music
winding its way through a maze of moods
with flowing fluidity and grace
they danced
flaying movements as skirt and foot moved
the quickness of the eye,
orange terracotta walls shine
wood jumped movements,
rhyme to sound, body and soul
move in and out of light
steel capped, high heeled, stilettos
danced, danced,
swirling energy, moved in and out
changing shape, transcending light
head straight body swealing
hands and arms move in unison
The gaiety of dance.

Victor John Grocock

The Start Of The Day

What do you think as you start your day?
Do you think or do you hope,
That things will go as you hope.

What do you think as you start your day?
Something positive or in a negative way.

What do you think as you start the day?
I'm going to make someone's life
Easier, that's my intention,
Sincerely I go without hesitation.

What do you think as you start the day?
Does your time allow you to pray?

That all goes well and the day is good,
Just thinking of helping others if we could,
For that's a special blessing
From which all should give,
Then every fresh day would
Be great to relive.

Carol Boneham

Nearer The Stars

To walk on clouds so soft and white
It's always better in the moonlight
To be nearer the stars I see at night
Shining and glistening to my delight
To be nearer the stars is a dream come true
When daylight comes I feel so blue.
But in the eve when dusk appears
I'm alive again and have no fears
To be nearer the stars.

G Deaves

The Walk . . . Or, Alzheimers

Yesterday, my mother and I hand in hand
against a blue and azure sky,
walk a path of early summer.
Dandelions, daisies abound,
trees in leaf, pre-nascent green,
and bird song full, fills the air.
We look around, the sun beats down.
One in coat, and hat and gloves.
One not. One in jeans, jersey, head, hands bare.
The day is hot.
My mother's world hems in around,
do we meet somewhere?

'Are you cold?'   'No Mum, are you . . . hot?'
'No . . . Are you tired?'   'No Mum, are you tired?'
'No . . . Are you cold?'   'No.'

For each to admit the other, would be to deny a fragile self,
our last hold on reality.

'Mother-daughter,' 'Daughter-mother . . .'
'You are my baby . . . I am your mother . . .'
'Yes Mum, you are my Mum, I am your daughter,
middle-aged, middle-spread but your 'baby' I am
and will be to no other.'

Our eyes meet, we laugh with the world,
the beauty of the day, and on my mother's face a look of love
I will find in no other.
Pointing to the way ahead, 'beautiful leaves,' she said . . .
'Yes Mum . . .' We sing 'our song'
'God in the sky, the sun is high, and 'all' is
very, very good,' 'Joy' in moment is enough.

A D M Thomas

Time To Reflect

Two clouds of dust have settled,
Two fires have now gone out.

Gemini twins are slowly rising,
Bringing forth dual emotives.

The orbit of this world has changed
Tremors spreading far and wide.

People seeking ways to unite
Minds newly focused on solutions.

Pondering the meaning of life and death
The value of freedom and democracy.

Multi-lateral consensus sought
As this world takes time to reflect.

Ian Barton

God Himself

The essence of retirement
does not mean to give up something,
but on the contrary it means to
foreclose one door and immediately
open another.
The doors that have in fact closed
are used doors, worn out doors,
door full of old ideas, but now the
retirement door has opened, a new
door full of new opportunities awaits
you to walk through it, into the
ideals that the future now holds.
Gone are the doors to the barren
land.
A change in ideals and outlook
awaits you, and time can change
attitudes to other things as well.
Inspirational epitaphs from the
panacea of past experiences can now
take place.   .
For in the instance of the epitaph
of the 'here's,' 'now's,' and
'wherefore's' of life, the time
has come for a new reappraisal of
one's acceptance unto God, the
Father of us all.
The Creator of that first and
last new door to the Alpha
and Omega of Life.
God Himself.

Anne Hadley

70

Friends

I have a richness buried in my heart:
A treasure manifold, yet marvellously simple.
It is the whispering presence of warm beings
Clustered within, exhaling patiently
Their love and inspiration into me.

Some have preceded me. They have gone before.
I may no longer see them on this earth . . .
And yet, they smile and live anon in me.
They influenced and changed me. Part of them
Is part of me. I am both one and yet diverse.

Many have marked my life. They gave so much.
To them I owe my silent growth, my opening out.
Many are still alive in my wide, personal world.
Some, I meet often, gratefully, eyes bright:
Communication's easy and relaxed.

With her, I laugh, enjoy her cheerful humour.
With him, I work, creating something fine.
With these, I help and serve and wait and listen,
With those, I'll sing, share music. Harmony!
With others still, converse and peacefully reflect.

I've friends for walking, drinking deep and strong
Draughts of green beauty in the countryside;
Friends with their families, wholesome and welcoming . . .
Friends from whose eyes, and in whose words, God shines
And calls me by my name, insistently, fondly.

Thankful am I, rejoicing and appreciative.
I relish cordial contact, letters - love . . .
Sure in the rocklike safety of support
I may rest quietly, growing year by year
And wish all blessings on my friends sincere.

Katharine Holmstrom

71

Personal Secrets

(Respectfully dedicated to both sides of the family)

There are all firmly rooted in my mind's eye.
For only I alone know the true depth of
These absolutely individual secrets.
For they come and go like ripples on a stream.
So you, yourself, cannot even begin to imagine both,
Widely and wildly, the innermost
Joys and anxieties which are all mine alone.

However, I will gladly share each one with you,
If only you will accordingly reciprocate.
So why don't you come and see me sometime?

M D H Stalker

I Remember It Well

Today's a day I reflect well,
My children come home again
After a long period apart,
Yes I had a mother's joy in my heart,
My son's my pride and joy
Singing songs he loves to hear
A lot of people listen to him sing
Say to me the pleasure he brings,
I remember and recall the best day of
All it's 17 years back now, I
Was a bride-to-be and my Mr
Right was waiting for me,
A lovely day was had, the weather
Was not bad, laughter galore, a
Man for me to adore and a future
Ahead together forever, so to this
Day I do reflect and remember it well,
I also remember days of sadness
And sorrow too, my father died and I
Was lost, alone with many a tear
Even now I remember it well.
I remember my son's birth
What a joy to his dad, his 1st child
And to have a family,
Oh what that meant to both
Him and me, a bundle of joy
Our dear little baby boy.
Oh yes I remember it well,
I'm blessed by it, all in my lifetime.
I remember it well.

Jo Willbye

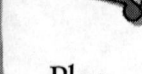

Play

Mum was very cross one day
I wanted to go out to play,
Oh! Please stop getting under my feet
You had better go out to play in the street:
So off I went with a hop and a skip
Calling aloud for my dog Pip!
Who bounced after me, with his tail a wagging,
And in his teeth his lead he was dragging.
Come on boy we will go for a walk
You can bark and I will talk.
He dropped his lead and grinned at me
We understand each other well as you can see.
Cherrio Mum, I'll be back for tea.
Out in the street we met our friend Steve
Who decided to come too, and leave
His friends, all playing tag
His Mother then wouldn't be able to nag
At the noise we were making if he wasn't there.
Also in the park there may be a fair.
If not Pip could run free,
We'd have plenty of fun, before time for tea.

P Wright

Praise The Lord - A Modern Psalm

Praise the Lord.
Praise God throughout the world;
Praise Him for all beauteous things.
Praise Him for His mighty act;
Praise Him for His great love.
Praise Him upon the pealing organ;
Praise Him with the piano and the guitar.
Praise Him with choruses and hymns;
Praise Him with your whole life.
I praise Him for His love for me;
I praise Him for His love for you.
Let all created things praise the Lord for
His enduring and unbeatable love.
Praise the Lord.

Joyce Allan

An Empty Heart

A southern Lass with a touch of class,
Yorkshire borders waited in earnest,
A fresh challenge of circumstance,
Childhood memories and family ties,
Old Farm Avenue left far behind.
For this beauty match lady,
Caring for others never stopped,
A motivated source of immense independence,
Grew and grew more in status,
Never stopping still,
Always something to be done,
That was our Mum!
Bold steps taken, White Rose for Red,
The Astell clan travels to Stockport town,
Here we truly settled down.
Classic Cinema films showing now,
Or at a certain Apex garage,
A loyal and hardworking cashier,
Warm and friendly with a welcome smile,
Greeted you from the best Mum in the world.
Sun soaked Spain, stray cats to feed,
Faded pictures of a much-loved holiday.
Problems shared of an open door,
Eager to listen time always found,
Worried and concerned,
More than anyone could imagine,
Personal pain no matter how bad forgotten,
With the words 'It does not matter'
Moving on is what we must do,
Without you Mum, it just will not be the same,
Becoming so difficult and hard,
Each day passing, a shed of tears everlasting,
Drained from an Ocean of Distress,
Your Fountain of Sacred Love.

A trembling hand lights a candle,
Watching a flame flickering of coldness felt,
Images of past life travel in the light,
White wax slowly melts and drips,
An Empty Heart,
Is all that is left,
As this message of love is sent.

Nigel Astell

Nanny Mac

I love you nan and always will,
although I didn't see you much.
I wish you could still be here
now, or that I could just see
you at least once more.
I miss visiting you and being
welcomed with open arms and smiles.
You really were a wonderful lady
who was always really kind and sweet.
I wish that you could see me
now and be there for me
whenever I need you. Although I
can't see you, I know that
you are always with me. You
will always have a place in my
heart and I will never ever
forget you nan. I miss you
really badly and hope you're happy
and reunited with grandad. I wish
I could have told you, just once,
how much I love you, but
now it's too late, so if you
are watching over me, I want
you to know that I do and I really
miss you. I will always remember you.

Phillip Carey

77

I Didn't Need To Ask

I didn't need to ask if He loved me
As He hung there on that tree,
I didn't need to ask Him how much
For it was plain for all to see.
I didn't need to see His face
For it was deeply etched with pain,
I didn't need to see the nail holes
As they took His body strain.

I don't need to ask Him why
He suffered there, just for me.
I don't need to ask Him when,
For I know it was *then* He set me free.
I don't know how to thank Him
For all that He has done,
But I'll try to live my life
Praising Father, Spirit, Son.

Geraldine Laker

Long Term World Partnership

The earth's beauty silent as light,
Shines with beauty from the sun's height.
The flowing sea sparkling and clear,
Makes music children love to hear.
The seasons' fruits and flowers share,
Their bounty for all folk who care.

Work force at home, in every sphere:
Where self-sacrifice is sincere,
Cheerfully use their highest powers;
Like master craftsmen's greatest hours.
Clear conscience leads to wisdom's way,
Crowns humane partnership each day.

In a world of terror and greed,
The weary cry in fear and need.
Guardians of justice, freedom, skill,
By enlightened concord fulfil;
Liberty when conflicts shall cease,
Harmony in bonds of peace.

Blest healing for the lonely soul,
Touching Jesus she was made whole.
Her trembling trust was not denied,
The Healer's mercies still abide.
His strong scarred hands lift those who fall,
Love's nearness meets dying rogue's call.

Sovereign Lord of earth and heaven,
Truth and power freely given;
Guide of nations diversity,
Lifts their sight to fraternity.
Gracious Spirit without measure,
Praise world's Maker, trustful treasure.

James Leonard Clough

The Tempest

Under the sway of the Tempest tune,
Clouds are racing across the moon,
Warning light from the lighthouse beam,
Torrential nightmare, the mariner's dream,
Nothing can stay in place, no one can sleep,
Afraid of a voyage to the angry deep,
As the waves rise higher over the deck line,
There's no time to think of your maiden's neckline.
For the sea is cruel, till the storm's abating,
They're praying and hoping and sighing and waiting.

Peter Buss

Hope

So many words have lost their meaning;
Long in danger 'hope' has lain.
Does it but mean 'delightful dreaming,'
Just a sop to ease the pain?
Just a gentle anaesthetic
To obscure reality?
Hope's not really so pathetic,
Hope is strong and true and free.
Hope is full of reassurance
Hope can challenge Death to sting,
Hope will toughen up endurance -
Winter vanquished by the spring.
Spring is sure, whatever harshness winter gales may bring;
So sure, by Easter's promise, is our reawakening.

Vaughan Stone

Bright And Beautiful

When I survey the brightness,
Of a springtime sky,
How fresh and green as spring flowers return,
With their colourful display.
For these are wonders dear Lord,
To give us joy and hope.
Never to deny its pleasures,
In the morning's simple sunlight.
For what is precious we must never forget,
Like the beauty all around us,
And the love that never fails.
But only within our hearts,
Can we see and feel the miracle of God's love,
Amid the beauty of these flowers,
Bringing us peace beyond our dreams from above.

Elisabeth Dill Perrin

These Things Give Pleasure

Things which give us pleasure today
are numerous in many a way
our children give us so much pleasure
when we play with them in our leisure.

Then there are our pets which give much joy
if we are a girl or boy
the cats are really very sweet
and the dogs, are going for a walk for a treat.

These things give us pleasure.

Then there is our shopping, can be fun these days
the sales give pleasure in many ways
when we see what is a bargain anyway
we decide to buy it and not delay.

Then when we are home and see the flowers starting to
bloom
we know the garden will be full of flowers soon
then there's the birds flying around
we get much pleasure when they make sounds.

These things give us pleasure.

So if we really want pleasure today
we know how to get it anyway
give love to those that we adore
then you can't wish for anything more.

Kay Taylor

83

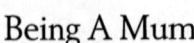

Being A Mum

Study hard, achieve your goals
Before you settle down
Do you really want to be mum
'Til your children are all grown
Children need you most
When they are very small
To love them and protect them
To be there when they call
Think hard about the future
Life is not a race
Be content with the life you choose
Don't moan 'I need my space'
You will still have time to do your thing
When your children leave the nest
Just be proud you are a mum
There will still be time to do the rest
You chose to have your children
So keep them safe and warm
Because it's you they will rely on
To keep them free from harm
So think before you have them
Have you got time to spare
Because children need their mum around
To give them tender loving care.

Shirley Edwards

Happiness Bottled

Wish I could take happiness, bottle it,
Each day I could sample a tiny bit.
I am praying this good feeling will last,
All ill-will should remain deep in my past.

I thought that true love might have passed me by,
On many nights about this I had cried.
Now I feel like a vibrant lover should,
Despair has all gone, for my life is good.

S Mullinger

Luminescent Hues

Luminescent hues, shimmer,
as a multi-coloured arc,
 thrusts, high,
 in misty rain.

Outstretched, to grasp
mocking sunbeams, as
black horses of clouds,
prance, across the sky.

Polly Davies

From The Heart Via The Biro

a circulation of one's thoughts, it was hard for us to talk to you
without you thinking that we were preaching.

An uninterrupted thought in print to a first born son.

to us you are no failure, your gifts you have left sideways for awhile
the excitement of your birth, the delight at every step, the sound
of word to ear and the production of that first tooth
I wondering what you would be at twenty one, the Crystal ball
I did not have to see, my dear.
The mind went wondering and you went with it, seeking the
excitement that's chemically released, a wild rose rambling.
We are still proud of you but now it's hard to show it.
We try to guide you back on the road, it's still too dull for you
for example, feeling the air on your face, the colour of the
sea, the simple beauty of the world holds no price tag, it's free.
When again you can see it, it has lost none of its appeal.
Count the gifts that you have got, these were given at your birth.
They are developed and are waiting to be used and only you
know when to start them off, when you are able to see what you
have got, you will be able to get whatever you will ever need.
Now you are close to thirty, find the strength to find you.
And the happiness will be yours, sermon over.

Margaret Gleeson Spanos

The Daffodils

I wandered lonely as a cloud
 That floats on high o'er vales and hills,
When all at once I saw a crowd,
 A host, of golden daffodils,
Beside the lake, beneath the trees,
Fluttering and dancing in the breeze.

Continuous as the stars that shine
 And twinkle on the milky way,
They stretched in never-ending line
 Along the margin of a bay:
Ten thousand saw I at a glance
Tossing their heads in sprightly dance.

The waves beside them danced, but they
 Out-did the sparkling waves in glee:
A Poet could not be but gay
 In such a jocund company!
I gazed - and gazed - but little thought
What wealth the show to me had brought:

For oft, when on my couch I lie
 In vacant or in pensive mood,
They flash upon that inward eye
 Which is the bliss of solitude;
And then my heart with pleasure fills,
And dances with the daffodils.

William Wordsworth

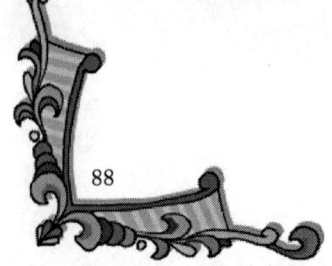

Written In Stone 1832

Your name, carved with love,
will last for centuries.
I hold the warm wood handle
to chisel the letter in the cold stone.
My hand trembles, let it be perfect,
as you would do it, father.
It is your memorial.
Mother would be proud to see
I have inherited your skill,
your patience,
patience to teach my son too,
for the family tradition to be carried on.
Perhaps he will carve happy-faced cherubs
like yours, father.
I cannot attempt them.
My decoration will be roses.
Mother loved pink roses.

Iris Long

Without You

What is missing now? I haven't got you
No one knows what I'm going through
Lost alone, does anyone care?
These feelings I have, I don't declare
When you lose the one you love
Only the lord knows up above
How long am I going to live? I wonder
Before I die and go up yonder
But until then, I think what will I do?
Because I cannot stop loving you
I know I must start to live and go on
Try to make my life happy again, this cannot be wrong
Every day my thoughts are of you
I always think if you were me, 'What would you do?'
Now I'm stuck here in what to say
Maybe I will learn what to do, some other day
Trying hard to find a life
Knowing what's wrong and what is right
At my age you would think I'd know
I hope one of these days soon, it will be so
Learning hard.

Anne Davey

Days Of Liberation

Through the prison walls of my mind
The light shines in.
The air from the window,
The sound that travels
Takes my soul, and sets me free.
When I seek the light -
The air and sound,
I find beauty and happiness
The skeleton in the cupboard diminish
The door is open.

Has my prison become my sanctuary?
I can rest here and find peace.
Let me remember where I am -
And feel
My higher power's presence
Enfolding me
In peace and light.

Sometimes the peace I seek deludes me
And lightning, from dark skies, pierces my
Heart, to reach, through pain and sorrow,
Into the deepest part
Where beauty lies
As a lily on still water.

That which makes me small and weak
Is the darkness in the mind that speaks.
You, who see me wise and strong
Sing the beauty in this song.

Light shines through and lets the colours play
Dissolves the set, dark shadows
Brings freedom and movement.

Barbro Pattie

91

Siren Song

I wandered by the sea today
where the cornfields kiss the shore
and seagulls cry by day but
owl hoots before dawn.

Tall grass, softly sway, on ocean
all their own
While just a whisper away white
capped waves do call.

In future will some record show
how the sea reclaimed its own
and tell how, golden cornfields drowned
beneath its raging scorn.

Nature is still master,
she's wilful, wild and strong
at your peril ignore her
wailing, siren song.

J Hubbard

You're Only As Old As You Feel

Morning comes, I try to rise,
My muscles ache from neck to
thighs.
The bed seems higher than a cliff,
My arms are weak, my legs are stiff.

Then as I stand and clean my teeth,
I look in the mirror and think 'Good
grief.'
A few more grey hairs have sneaked
in,
And they're just the new ones on
my chin.
The silver strands upon my head,
Are filling me with fear and dread.

Beneath my bloodshot eyes are
bags,
My cheeks have dropped and my
chin sags.
I cover my face with magic cream,
For it to work is just a dream.

The scales are lurking on the floor,
I push them back behind the door.
I've had enough shocks for one day,
'Tomorrow I'll slim again,' I say.
'And then I'll proudly stand on
you,
You won't beat me, I'll starve if I have
to.'

My legs resemble old street maps,
The purple veins stand out like caps.

Limbs that once were tanned
and fatless,
Now resemble a Collins Atlas.

The fact that still my teeth are real,
Doesn't help the way I feel.
My pearly jewels that once were white,
Would enhance Metal Mickey's bite.

I've tried so hard to kick the fags,
But comfort comes in long deep drags.
My lungs are calling in despair,
'Please give us lots of clean fresh air.
Give up the weed, we'll help you cope,
Stop smoking now, don't be a dope.'

These frets have caused one more hot flush,
My face has gone from white to blush.
I'm sick of hormones playing tricks,
I don't know how they get their kicks
From telling me, 'You're getting old,'
By blowing hot then blowing cold.
Surely there's a kinder way
Of saying, 'Girl you've had your day.'

And then I think, 'It's not the end,'
It's not worth going round the bend.
It's how you feel inside that counts,
That inward glow that makes me
bounce.
The glow that comes from being *me,*
Forget the mirror, 'Set me free!'

M Meredith

Violet

(In memory of Violet Meakin)

If ever I was ill, I'd visit her home
Over the fields where the cows would roam
She'd sit by the fire and greet me forthwith
Her house always warm, the way that she lived.

We would sit and watch old black and white films
I'd sit by the fire warming my limbs
My coldness would go, my aching subside
I'd talk to her and admire her pride.

The smell of tobacco and freshly washed clothes
The food in the kitchen on top of the stove
House always warm such a nice place to stay
Even that briefly while my fever went away.

I'd have dinner and a hot mug of tea,
She'd sit and chat about how things used to be
I still miss her now all these years down the line
My grandma was lovely, she treated me fine.

Steven Pape

Thoughts On Life

*(Dedicated to dear John Stephens who
always encouraged me with my poetry)*

Picture the blossom on the apple tree
So pretty and pink a beauty to see,
Then searching you'll find the tiny fruit
Bursting into shape from its mother root.

Listen to the sky larks singing on high,
And the blackbird's song as he waits nearby
To grab a meal as the soil is turned,
Returning to the nest, supper well earned.

Think of the animals upon this earth
Puppies and kittens you have seen given birth,
The life of creatures both great and small
Has Mother Nature embracing them all.

Hold a new baby so little and sweet
With tiny fingers and nails complete,
The miracle of life comes from God above
He enfolds everyone in His infinite love.

Peggy Courteen

Desiderata

Go placidly amid the noise and haste
and remember what peace there may be in silence.
As far as possible without surrender, be on good terms with all persons.
Speak your truth quietly and clearly and listen to others,
even the dull and ignorant; they too have their story.
Avoid loud and aggressive persons; they are vexations to the spirit.
If you compare yourself with others you may become vain or bitter,
for always there will be greater and lesser persons than yourself.
Enjoy your achievements as well as your plans.
Keep interested in your career, however humble;
it is a real possession in the changing fortunes of time.
Exercise caution in your business affairs,
for the world is full of trickery.
But let this not blind you to what virtue there is.
Many persons strive for high ideals
and everywhere life is full of heroism.
Be yourself.
Especially do not feign affection.
Neither by cynical about love,
for in the face of all aridity and disappointment
it is s perennial as the grass.
Take kindly the counsel of the years,
gracerful surrendering the things of youth.
Nurture strength of spirit to shield you in sudden misfortune.
But do not distress yourself with imaginings.
Beyond a wholesome discipline be gentle with yourself.
You are a child of the universe no less than the trees and the stars.
You have the right to be here.
And whether it is clear to you or not,
no doubt the universe is unfolding as it should.

Therefore be at peace with God,
whatever you conceive him to be,
and whatever your labours and aspirations in the noisy confusion of life,
keep peace with your soul.
With all its sham and drudgery and broken dreams
it is still a beautiful world.
Be cheerful. Strive to be happy.

Max Ehrman

The Tragic Comedy

My teddy bear is not enough
My loving embrace, filled . . . with fluff!
My tearful eyes meet plastic bumps
My hopes beat into soft clumps of lumps.

Love is not always an enjoyable game
Lust, not a perpetual night time play
So why so willingly accommodate this change
Because when love dawns . . . *everything* is forgotten.

Rachel Abbey

This Day

This very day I pray heaven look on me
With tender grace, may your spirit be kind
In the way it would, I need to know you have loving care
That I can turn to you both night and day, should I ever
Feel alone, I pray take that fear away from me, draw
Me close, let me understand you are there, may I in
Return sing your praise to heaven! Heights tell my world
How I feel, inside of me, your words are wonderful as
My searching eyes tell my heart, man on earth will never
Replace your works of art, you alone give life to every
Living soul, all creation is from your loving creative hands.
I request when I am having my own moments of passing
Doubts about myself, will you by your tender grace,
Let me know in some way, I have a value in your eyes,
That you gave the gift of life to me, I was a part of your
Working plans, in return let me sing your endless praise.

R Scannell

Another Time Another Place

Another time, another place, the wind would be fondling
Audibly, the palm tree fronds, on the shore.
We'd hear the sound of the sea lapping rhythmically.
Waves reminding me of the sound of breathing, tossed out,
Exhalations, crashing ashore, onto the finest sand.
Then - as with the taking in of a deep breath, the sea,
Sounding to be swept back out again, with a sigh, ecstatic.
There'd be the sound of crickets chattering -
And t'would be like the stars could be heard twinkling.
And if our hearing were to be very good, perhaps,
We'd even hear the crabs dancing in the moonlight,
At the water's edge!

Rosemary Wamba

Beautiful Moon

I looked for you among the clouds
of drifting wisps of light and could
not find you but I knew you had to
be there, somewhere. I knew you could
not just leave on a whim.

Barely noticed amongst the sun's
last rays of the evening I watched
and waited until at last on a
burst of sunlight I spotted you.
Your semicircular shape almost invisible.

And as sunset drew closer, your
presence is seen peeping behind a
gossamer cloud. Swirling formations
of cloud on a perfect blue sky.

Your face begins to glisten as
you too catch the sun's rays, only your
basking will be in our darkness.

How better to watch you and
marvel at your sparkling landscape.
Did man set foot on you? Oh, if only
he had let you alone, you would
still be perfect.

Susie J Burnette

Pain

I wish I could take the pain away,
The pain you so bravely bear,
I wish I could take the pain away,
So your life could be without care.

If only I could take the pain away,
So we could sit and enjoy the flowers,
If only I could take the pain away,
We could talk for hours and hours.

But no I cannot take the pain away,
No matter how hard I may try,
But no I cannot take the pain away,
Just cry, just cry, just cry.

Geraldine Giles

This Is God

I followed the path, listening to
droplets pattering through the
hedges and trees.
Mist rested in the vale, peppering
the view, silent image, time had
avoided, left alone, protected.
Huge skies kissed the earth
with gentle precision, bold
blues and troubled clouds
had all given me their show.
Now the sun would melt through,
sparkling the pools and droplets.
The soaked wildflowers began
to raise their heads from the
heavy fall.
The biting scent of the fields
carried me on my wander, passed
the oak tree where someone had
nailed a sign, 'This is God.'
I looked into the vale at the
church spires pointing into
turquoise and thought that
they could be right.

Hilary Vance

102

Easter Reflection

What would you do if your leader and best friend was murdered?

What would you do if his murderers came looking for you to kill you?

What would you do if 3 days later one or two of your friends said, 'He is alive we've seen him?'

What would you do? Would you believe or doubt?

What would you do if you then saw him yourself, not only you, but up to 500 others at one time also and over the next 40 days he ate with you again, talked with you again?

He explained the reason he had to die in that way.

He explained he was born into the world for that very reason!

And he knew all these things were going to happen and accepted them.

What would you do when it dawned on you, who your friend really was?

What would you do when it really dawned on you who this man was?

His name is Jesus Christ, he is the Son of God.

He was given for you.

Ask yourself, 'What does this mean?'

What would you do?

Would you be willing to die for a lie if you knew all this to be untrue? No

This is how the Christian church started.

Many people say they believe in God.

The Holy Bible says demons believe in God and tremble (James 2.9)

If all paths lead to God, Jesus came and Died for nothing.

The Holy Bible says, 'For God so loved the world that he gave his only begotten Son that whoever believes in Him should not perish but have everlasting Life.'

Grasp what all this means, it's important for you and relevant today.

Richard Knights

Respite

He feints, swivelling neatly,
striking the ball on the rise,
turning as it enters the net.
Punching air, he leaps skywards,
his features drained of tension.

It is not a new experience,
just one he's learned to savour,
as each year slips quickly by.
A quick fix, an instant remedy,
but no less the welcome for that.

He runs to the crowd, ecstatic,
grateful to share his relief.
Happy to have thwarted that
spectre called time, before it
brandishes the red card, forever.

Paul Kelly

Morning

First light, my light.
Others eyes firmly shut, no need to share.
Gone the black night.
Absorb with hunger the new air.

First sun, my sun.
Others have the warmth of bedding, no need to
share.
Gone the cold night.
Absorb with hunger all things dear.

First daydreams, my daydreams.
Others will think of the day's dollar, no need to
share.
Gone the nightmare scenes.
Absorb with hunger the white knight to care.

First plans, my plans.
Others will hurry and scurry, no time to share.
Gone the night's idleness.
Absorb the hunger to leave your mark here.

Erica Sillett

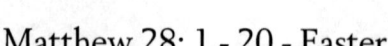

Matthew 28: 1 - 20 - Easter

1. In the end of the Sabbath, as it began to dawn toward the first day of the week, came Mary Magdalene and the other Mary to see the sepulchre.

2. And, behold, there was a great earthquake: for the angel of the Lord descended from heaven, and came and rolled back the stone from the door, and sat upon it.

3. His countenance was like lightning, and his raiment white as snow:

4. And for fear of him the keepers did shake, and became as dead men.

5. And the angel answered and said unto the women, Fear not ye: for I know that ye seek Jesus, which was crucified.

6. He is not here: for he is risen, as he said, Come, see the place where the Lord lay.

7. And go quickly, and tell his disciples that he is risen from the dead; and behold, he goeth before you into Galilee; there shall ye see him: lo, I have told you.

8. And they departed quickly from the sepulchre with fear and great joy; and did run to bring his disciples' word.

9. And as they went to tell his disciples, behold, Jesus met them, saying, All hail. And they came and held him by the feet, and worshipped him.

10. Then said Jesus unto them, Be not afraid: go tell my brethren that they go into Galilee, and there shall they see me.

Troubles Shared

We met just at the corner
I said, 'Good morning how are you?'
'Indeed" she said, 'I don't feel well
I think I've got the flu
My head is simply aching
And my legs just feel like lead
I have to go out to the shop.
But should really be in bed.'
I said, 'I'm very sorry
But I have to hurry on
I'm going to a meeting
So I'll have to run along.'
She said, 'My eyes are dimming
And my hair is going thin
And now I've lost my glasses
I've probably put them in the bin.'
I said, 'I really must get on
I'm going to be late,'
But she said, 'I haven't told you
Of this other turn of fate.
My neighbour's dog has chased my cat
And still she's not come back,
My husband took time off from work
And now has got the sack.'
She said, 'My feet are hurting now
For my shoes have pinched my toes,'
I thought next time we met
I'll say a very quick 'Hello!'

Doreen Todd

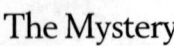

The Mystery

The grand piano stood solid on the floor,
Placed there a velvet covered stool,
With not a soul in sight the ivory keys were playing,
The chandelier above reflecting brilliant light,
But there was just a ghostly shadow
transparent it would seem come back to
haunt the old place from days gone by,
at last the music fades away and the old
Grand Piano stands silent once again.

Olive M Poole

Love

Love is a thing which can't be bought,
Love is a thing which should be taught,
Love is a thing which helps the distraught,
Love is a wonderful thing.

Love is a thing for fathers and mothers,
Love is a thing for sisters and brothers,
Love is a thing we should give to others,
Love is a beautiful thing.

Love is a thing for both strong and weak,
Love is a thing of which we should speak,
Love is a thing we all should seek
Love is a glorious thing.

Love is a thing for all mankind,
Love is a thing which hasn't declined,
Love is a thing for peace of mind,
Love is the only thing.

W Papworth

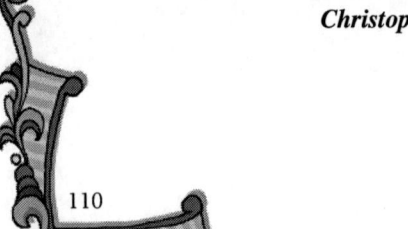

Woodland Harbingers

Primrose

From undisturbed seclusion 'midst the tangle
Of long-grounded boughs and last year's lifeless leaves
There shines out in a strong determined hue
That ancient pointer to the forest's age
Which e'en before its pillars lofty grew
Stippled the temple floor with flecks of gold
The glowing-out-of-dimness trim primrose.

Windflower

Ring the woodland changes now
And let the glades of forest-virgin snow
The Milky Way white wood anemones
Thaw spring's chill and spartan symmetry
Into softer lines of emerald leafy loveliness
And let creation's new life find a myriad forms
Reflecting Him whose spirit knows no bounds.

Bluebell

The shy-at-first sheer mesmeritic haze
Unlaid brush-stroke of celestial hue
Shapes now into those carillons of praise
Whose silent chimes ring out perspectives new
And fast transform the landscape's slate-grey face
Into a Van Gogh palette of vibrating blue
Glade-gathered glimpses of God's boundless grace.

Christopher Rudd

A Bad Day

My faith is weak
But sometimes strong
Remembering that helps me sleep
When my faith is strong
I remember the 'one' who
Rewarded me when my faith
Is weak, that sometimes it is strong.

Michael Lyth

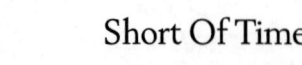

Short Of Time

It's a well known fact
As we journey through life
That we are always 'short of time'.

The list of things
That we think that we should do
Gets longer 'all the time'.

The older we get,
The harder we try
In our effort to 'save time'.

But at the end of our life
The list is still there
And we are surely very 'short of time'.

Rosemary Millard

Contentment

The smell of clean washing
Just off the line,
A warm fire, with family fine.
Thanks for a meal, I've cooked
A comment on the way I looked.

A loving hug before I get up
Cup of tea in a china cup
A hymn sung with feeling
Something with meaning.
Simple pleasures.

Life-long treasures
Books to read
A family to feed
Without a care
Here in my chair.

S Draper

Hymn To Love

Oh my love what joy you bring me when within your arms entwined
Whispered words of sweet ecstasy bid me leave the world behind
Body warm and softly clinging feeling heartbeats heart on heart
Every nerve and muscle singing longing for us ne'er to part
Tears that make the joy ecstatic tears that no one can explain
Such emotion enigmatic craving more to soothe the pain
Then with all the passion sated softly lain across my breast
Tousled hair and pain abated sink into a peaceful rest
Watching you my love and seeing that so lovely thing is mine
Feeling love flow through my being like intoxicating wine
Oh to God whatever sending that I may when life is done
Feel your kisses never ending hold you ever dearest one.

E J Urmston

Untitled

When first you wake,
And open your eyes,
When you look in the mirror,
And think you're disguised,
You would dearly love to return to bed,
And on that pillow rest your head,
But you must wash and dress instead,
To prepare yourself for the day ahead.

Not knowing what's in store today,
Off you go along your way,
But be warned and don't delay,
Time is running away each day.

So grab your moments with both hands,
And make every second count,
Enjoy your happiness when on your lap it lands,
If only a tiny amount,
You never know how long it will last,
Or when your time will end,
So embrace this life as a whole,
Yourself, family and friend.

Sue Watson

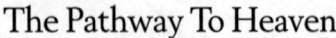

The Pathway To Heaven

There is a God, we know it's true,
He's looking after me and you,
When trouble comes stay nice and calm,
Or read the Bible, or a psalm,
God is close to us through life,
And through trouble, toil and strife,
When friends desert you, never fear,
God is by you, day and year,
Angels guard us night and day,
We must to God always pray,
To help us through the stony ways,
Of life's hard knocks and unfair ways,
God will guard us, till the end,
And keep us safe from foe and friend,
God will say - you've done so well,
With me in happiness you will dwell.

Elizabeth Woodham

Freedom

'Don't catch that butterfly - it'll only die'
They told me - 'let it have a life, let it fly
Its time here is so very, very short
If trapped its beauty fades - then mort
So leave it to enjoy flying wild and free
Its fate not for us to control - just for us to see . . .'

Caren Taylor

Silent Comfort

One day when I was sad
She took my hand and made me glad

One day she wiped away a tear
And took away all my fear

One time she stayed all through the night
Just in case I took a fright

She never spoke a single word
Nothing needed to be heard

Carol Sheppard

The Clod And The Pebble

'Love seeketh not itself to please,
 Nor for itself hath any care,
But for another gives its ease,
 And builds a heaven in hell's despair.'

So sung a little clod of clay,
 Trodden with the cattle's feet,
But a pebble of the brook
 Warbled out these metres meet:

'Love seeketh only Self to please,
 To bind another to its delight,
Joys in another's loss of ease,
 And builds a hell in heaven's despite.'

William Blake

You Passed On By

You left me bleeding,
Ignored my pleading,
A gaping wound in my heart.

You left me lying,
Don't leave me dying,
Drowning in tears that still smart.

So much inner pain,
Was it all in van,
Giving, not counting the cost?

There's nowhere to rest
With a troubled breast,
Only sense of what's lost.

No one is to blame
Following false aim,
It's part of life's long learning.

The right path to bliss
Is easy to miss
Pursuing endless burning.

Love ever roams free,
Though striving to be
Entangled with another.

Happiness is brief,
Which soon turns to grief,
Joyfulness somewhere other.

Worship of a star
Is best from afar,
Seeking to reach contentment.

Everlasting things
True joy with it brings,
Love, the greatest attainment.

Betty Mealand

Silence

Night-time falls, quiet again
no visitors to call
just myself remains
with memories of yesterday
and friends past
of days that are endless
yet never seem to last

My family all grown
and moved away
children of their own
time occupied with work and play

No time to dwindle
on getting old
my time is here
my future foretold.

Dawn Miller

Spring

Sinks the sun beneath the distant haze
And hurries day towards predestined doom,
Its joyful colours fast submerged in gloom.
The end of days?
So, winter too appears to play the king
Deceiving prostrate Nature he's the master of the earth
While She prepares in silence and in darkness her rebirth;
Comes on the spring!
So, with such powerful witnesses before our eyes
As morning every day and spring's repeated splendour,
How can we fail to grasp God's infinite agenda
And welcome that great spring when we ourselves shall rise?
Where is Death's sting? O, where indeed,
When buried lies the living seed?

Vaughan Stone

Idle Thoughts

I got up this morning, willing to do
A lot of chores and things.
But then I sat down, and thought them all through,
That's what daydreaming brings.

I'm not that lazy, and like to do well,
And work quite hard at times,
But maybe I'm slowing up, who can tell?
Time regulates the chimes.

All of my days, are flying by so fast,
Trying to stay with life.
I've done most things, I wanted, in the past,
Sometimes I've had some strife.

But life has been good to me, I must say.
Coping from day to day,
Being lucky, in an unlucky way,
Wishing good health will stay.

It's strange how elastic time seems to go,
Changing within your mind.
Going quick, when you want it to go slow,
And vice versa find.

Well, here is the start to another week,
With lots of things to see,
Today is fine, with happiness to seek,
Guess, it's all meant to be!

D Ranson

Mum And Dad

I remember when I was just a kid
All the love you gave me, all the things you did
It must have been a hard life
To clothe and feed us all
But together you achieved it
With your backs against the wall.
I often sit and think of you
And wished I'd asked you more
About your lives, your hopes and dreams
There were many I am sure.
It's only now I'm older
With children of my own
I sit and think about you
And all the hardship you must have known.
I wish I'd showed you more
How I cared for both of you
I feel deep in my heart
That you both really knew.
And as the years go by
I think more about the past
So proud you were my parents
Who gave me memories made to last.

Shirley Edwards

SchÖnleit, Austria

For such a moment
What price would the princes dare to pay
That could afford a glimpse of your serenity?

The giants falter, and
Fall weak upon their knees -
While you smile
The sun, at the corner of your mouth
Casts a bright beam of light across your rocky face.

Yet I do not fear you.
For I, as a child
Splash and paddle in the
Tears of laughter
At your feet.

Whilst high above,
Your peaked brow
Watches over me.

Mark Hopkins

Sylvia

You are always there for someone else
Never thinking of yourself,
You listen to their tales of woe
And point them down which road to go.

You listen to them from the start
The advice you give is from the heart
No matter what these people ask
You do it for love, not a task
And when the day comes to an end
They stop and think well she is our friend,

But what they do not realise
That behind your kindness, that you hide
Things that you could only know
And that you don't want your sadness to show
I wonder if they only knew

Would they do the same for you.

D A C

Just A Thought

Inspiration is a great healer
It lifts us up from boredom
Self pity - sorry for ourselves
It gives us ideas which
We could achieve
It gives us insight we
Never thought existed
Have a go

J Campbell Jones

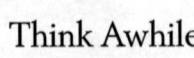

Think Awhile

Think of all the things in life
 That always give you pleasure,
Then think of all the memories
 That you will always treasure
A certain smile, a needed hug
 Can help you carry on
You'll even shed a little tear when
 You hear a certain song.
Never take love for granted
We've got to be shown and told,
To love and be loved is life itself
And it's worth its weight in gold.
Happiness is Heaven sent
It's yours, if you will be content.

J Lowe

Stargazing

And did those stars in time long gone
shine down on Earth's warm sphere
encouraging all those myriad specks of
life to burgeon forth.
Escape from the arms of their clinging brothers
to strive and fight to conquer this planet.
These sightless mindless grains of
energy first covered themselves in a
skin of their own, to save and conserve
their inner strength. To suckle and
nurture their plan of the future.
And did these life forms turn to the
light warmed by the day and the magic
of night.
And form little windows that their
intelligence might grow.
By continually conquering and absorbing
the energy of their kind.
Existing for aeons until existence
became life?

Marjorie Matthews

What Price?

How much does it cost
Just once in a while
To wish someone good day
And give them a smile?
What price a kindness
Or to offer a hand
To show a poor soul
That you do understand?
No time or money
To help someone old
But to them and the lonely
It's worth a pot full of gold.

J O'Donoghue

I'm There

Can you see the tear in my eye?
I want to hold it back, I really try
But my love for you it is so strong
It's in my heart that you belong

And when you feel down,
It's my tears that will drown
Your hurt, your pain, your sorrow.
My tears they're true
And show love for you.
You and I will fight
And we will see the light,
Through each day

Can you hear the sound of weeping?
The thoughts of you my mind is keeping.
Every day and every night
You're the one that's in my sight.

You know that I am always there
And at my heart you can tear.
If you feel pain in your mind
It's me that you should come and find.

Ally Moore

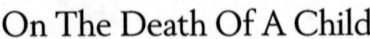

On The Death Of A Child

Weep not for me, for I am safe now,
and will live my life in eternal youth.
Rather mourn the lost years.
Years of youthful exuberance
that then take on adults more sober mantle
and then the serenity of senior years.
Mourn for children that might have been.
I am close and sense your sorrow and pain,
and when that sorrow and cruel pain ease,
as ease they must in the fullness of time,
then remember me with love and joy,
and think on the good times that we had.
When your life's circle is complete
and the sands of time are running out,
then at Heaven's Gate for you I'll wait,
to take your hand and lead you home.

Cathy Franklin

Shadows Of Words

Don't be insulted by useless goals.
Throw off their control,
Allow them to fall and shatter.
Feeble aims are worthless,
Like frost under sun.

Think deeply, in silence.
Promote kindness and the
Welfare of others.
A charitable heart will
Yield fruit in season.

Despise violence; be sturdy
In the sight of proud men.
Flattering words deceive
And cannot be trusted, each
Syllable a plot of ruin.

Pursue lies; drive confusion away.
Judge in favour of right. Be keenly
Troubled by betrayal, silver
Tongues and helpless friends.
Be unfailing in goodness.

Examine your heart; perfect
Deeds and dependable
Words - perfect. The heart
Is their stronghold.
Do good; secure honour.

Hidden faults and silent speeches
Make victims of all. Damp pillows
Reveal compassion; be valid,
Create and gather.
Weeping shortens life.

And life is one beat of butterfly wings,
Death a paradise of winters;
A forever kingdom, eternal.
Be humble - its ten thousand
Doorways are wide, and always open.

133

Tony Cullen

Constant Companion

'I will not leave thee, nor forsake thee',
Thus saith my Father's Word.
Though storm clouds lower, shine or shower,
I have His promise - He watches over me.

He walks beside me through winter's storms
Or summer's cloudless day.
Though footsteps falter He does not alter -
I have His promise: It will last for aye.

Can I, by nature sinful, lost, defiled,
Even now to God be reconciled?
His promise stands - repent, believe,
And even now His Peace receive.

No more alone Life's toilsome road to tread!
He lives, the King, Who once was dead!
Though worldlings scoff, He changes not.
What joy to know He loves me so.

Oh! Thou Who art my Refuge, Rock and Guide
Teach me to flee to Thee and hide;
Until the storms of Life all safely past,
I rest in Thee; safe Home at last.

Olive M Spurgeon

Hamlet

Act 1 Sc 3

Polonius to his son Laertes.

Give thy thoughts no tongue,
Nor any unproportioned thought his act.
Be thou familiar, but by no means vulgar.
Those friends thou hast, and their adoption tried,
Grapple them to thy soul with hoops of steel;
But do not dull thy palm with entertainment
Of each new-hatch'd, unfledged comrade. Beware
Of entrance to a quarrel, but being in,
Bear't that the opposed may beware of thee.
Give every man thy ear, but few thy voice;
Take each man's censure, but reserve thy judgement.
Costly thy habit as thy purse can buy,
But not express'd in fancy; rich, not gaudy;
For the apparel oft proclaims the man,
And they in France of the best rank and station
Are of a most select and generous chief in that.
Neither a borrower nor a lender be;
For loan oft loses both itself and friend,
And borrowing dulls the edge of husbandry.
This above all: to shine ownself be true,
And it must follow, as the night the day,
Thou canst not then be false to any man.

William Shakespeare

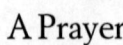

A Prayer

I will say a prayer for you
And ask the Lord above
To lay His healing hands on you
And shower you with His love
I know that God will listen
To what I have to say
And if it is His will
He may heal you on this day
I must not be complacent
And think that God will do
All the things I ask Him
He may have plans for you
So I will keep on praying
And thank the Lord above
For all His gifts of goodness
For all His perfect love

Mary Turner

The Path Of The Unknown

Throughout the night she sleeps
Her dreams, she dreams so meek
She wakes up to the still morning
Afresh she feels, the new day begins

The medley in her head she can't hide
Something she always starts the day with
Starts her journey through the path
Of the unknown.

Julie Mitchell

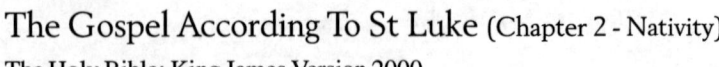

The Gospel According To St Luke (Chapter 2 - Nativity)

The Holy Bible: King James Version 2000

1. And it came to pass in those days, that there went out a decree from Caesar Augustus, that all the world should be taxed.
2. (And this taxing was first made when Cyre'ni-us was governor of Syria.)
3. And all went to be taxed, every one into his own city.
4. And Joseph also went up from Galilee, out of the city of Nazareth, into Judea, unto the city of David, which is called Bethlehem, (because he was of the house and lineage of David.)
5. to be taxed with Mary his espoused wife, being great with child.
6. And so it was, that, while they were there, the days were accomplished that she should be delivered.
7. And she brought forth her firstborn son, and wrapped him in swaddling clothes, and laid him in a manger; because there was no room for them in the inn.

The Shepherds and the Angels
8. And there were in the same country shepherds abiding in the field, keeping watch over their flock by night.
9. And, lo, the angel of the Lord came upon them, and the glory of the Lord shone round about them; and they were sore afraid.
10. And the angel said unto them, Fear not: for, behold, I bring you good tidings of great joy, which shall be to all people.
11. For unto you is born this day in the city of David a Saviour, which is Christ the Lord.
12. And this shall be a sign unto you; Ye shall find the babe wrapped in swaddling clothes, lying in a manger.
13. And suddenly there was with the angel a multitude of the heavenly host praising God, and saying,
14. Glory to God in the highest, and on earth peace, good will toward men.

Thoughts

Reach out and hold a piece of Heaven
Clasp it in your hand
It is a priceless treasure
Only given on God's command
Who could then be frightened
Who could turn away
After sharing the joy and peace
Of that first Christmas Day.

Elizabeth Caswell

I Should Like To . . .

I should like to touch the icy clouds on a cold, grey winter's
morning;
I would like to paint the trumpet of an elephant, far away on
the steaming Savannah of Africa;
I should like to hear the pain of a pebble, trampled upon by
many feet over the years;
I would love to keep the howl of a wolf in a jar, from under-
neath the moon on the vast prairie;
I should like to understand the mighty ravens' cry from up on
top of tall church spire;
I would like to listen to the vivid colours on a butterfly's
wings, flitting from flower to flower;
I should like to feel the roar of pride from a lion, pouncing on its prey;
I should like to take home the call of an eagle, swooping in for the kill;
I should like to see the thunder on a stormy night, breaking the silence;
I should like to taste the sweetness of a flower.

Martin Samson

One More Star In The Sky

One more angel in heaven.
One more star in the sky.
You were gone without a trace.
And still we wonder why.
Why you felt you had no life.
Why you felt such pain.
Why the world was in a spin.
Avoiding the constant rain.
The rain you felt was on your side.
When everything else would fall.
You'd stand back up and find your ground,
Without a stutter or stall.
One day that rain, it got too much.
It washed away your pride.
Washed away your only hope.
Made all your dreams collide.
As from there we have no clue.
Have no reasoning why.
There's one more angel in heaven.
One more star in the sky.

Laura Heywood

Reflections Of Life

Before we are born, our future is planned,
And not by God's almighty hand,
Our path may be paved, but it's ours to steer,
We have lessons to learn, is that why we are here!
As we travel along our road of life
Our chosen way, may be filled with strife,
We can wander aimlessly, or fall from the track,
And suffer great hardships, on our way back,
To some life's road must seem endlessly long,
For they cannot find, where they belong,
Born to exist, in cruelty and fear
They must surely ask, 'Why am I here?'
And yet their souls struggle to survive,
Suffering each day, just to stay alive,
Some souls are blessed, with a life at ease
The world is theirs, to do as they please,
Everything they touch, seems to turn to gold
They are never hungry, lost, or cold,
Some are born leaders, others born to be led,
Others are gifted, with a knowledge inbred,
Then there's the poor, the needy, the slow,
Never knowing which way, they should go,
We are here for a purpose, to live out our lives,
With each of us sending out, different vibes,
Help me, love me, we all have our needs,
And whether rich or poor, each of us bleeds,
Disease and illness can inflict such pain,
We all suffer grief, no matter what our fame,
No money, nor power, can save a soul
When our time is done, death takes it toll!

Pat Scott

142

Our Day

Let nothing upset or distress us
In this mad busy world today
Each time we wake to greet the morn
We should all reflect and pray
That we *can* get up in the morning
That we *can* in fact just walk
That we *can* do things for ourselves
That we *can* see and hear and talk
Without all these simple things in life
We would find it so very hard.
Therefore we should always remember
There are thousands of us who can't
Walk, talk or hear or see at all
We must be thankful in every way
We must not let ourselves get downhearted
But get up! And get on with *our day.*

Margaret Luckett-Curtis

Luke 24: (Ascension)

50. And he led them out as far as to Bethany, and he lifted up his hands, and blessed them.

51. And it came to pass, while he blessed them, he was parted from them, and carried up into heaven.

52. And they worshipped him, and returned to Jerusalem with great joy:

53. And were continually in the temple, praising and blessing God. Amen.

The Gift Of Sight

Oh what a wonderful thing it is to be able to see,
All nature's finery,
The trees, flowers, seas and mountains but to name a few
both
Living and dying and re-born in season after season,
And of course the skies changing as it does,
People with happy faces and sad ones, eclipses of the sun,
Rainbows and its many colours, which regularly occur,
Falling snowdrifts that turn everything white bringing a new
Sparkle to the light,
Such is the glory of the gift of sight.

Barry Dubber

Morning

Softly, step softly,
The morning is sighing
Whispering sunrise, the shadows are flying
Murmuring breezes awaken the river
Now bathed in pure light of sunshine and silver.

Gently, step gently,
Disturb not the dewdrops.
Hark now, a sweet sound is heard in the tree tops,
Birds of the air singing songs of the morning,
Praising the beauty as new day is dawning.

Gathering strength now
The morning is singing,
Filled with the sounds of a million things living,
A million new lives that the sunshine is forming -
Be glad that you've witnessed the birth of a morning.

Silently, silently,
Live through your senses,
Forget all your acts and the foolish pretences,
Let go of your heart, let it fly with the swallow,
Rejoice in today, let there be no more sorrow.

Dorothy Kemp

Probably

What of the future, what will it bring?
Will song birds still be free to sing?
Will sheep and shepherds still be seen?
On rolling hills of emerald green.

Maybe.

Will Everest still command respect?
As of't her highest walls reject
Those climbers seeking out its tor
Will we still hear Niagara's roar?

Perhaps.

What of the starving and homeless creed?
Will there still be more mouths to feed?
Will clergy on their knees still pray,
For wretched sinners?

Who can say?

I asked our Lord who's will be thine
The answers to these thoughts of mine
He smiled with eyes that held no fear
Then whispered softly in my ear.

I think so, yes I think so.

Roy Goodswen

Weeds

Weeds! I never knew they could grow so fast,
Out in the garden, it's dry at last.
Pulled up a barrowful, didn't take long,
Four days later another batch up, still looking strong.

Will I ever be rid of the little devils,
Course I could let them grow, instead of flowers.
Then I need not spend so many wasted hours
Clearing the ground for my flower seed,
After all, what is a weed?

Only a flower not cultivated,
Very proliferous, and motivated.
Towards the survival of the fittest,
Just look at the dandelion, really very pretty
And very welcome in my ditty.

But then daisies are pretty too!
What about buttercups? I've pulled up a few,
And the bluebells, they're just a wild flower,
But they've been cultivated, and can be bought
And they multiply practically from nought.

So after a few years, you have a good show
And a bunch tied with ribbon with a big bow,
Is a very nice present to put on the table,
Especially if the recipient is not able
To go to the woods to see them in bloom,
But to have a bunch brought to their room,
Would be very much appreciated.

P Wright

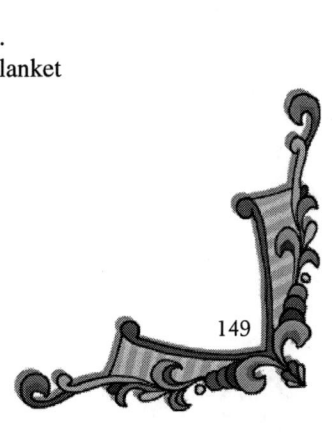

Nature's Comforts

All around is green, yellow, auburn.
Grass buttercups.
Trees with golden brown leaves,
Dark grungy bark,
Roots trudging into soil,
Weaving a path to visit Mother's core.

Up above is blue, white, grey.
Hydrogen clouds,
Sunshine rays drenching the air,
Lazy in haze.
Rain promises pots of gold wrapped in bows,
The colours sing a lullaby.

Darkness falls, purple, brown, black.
Where does it land?
It reflects in the moving, soothing sea
And ancient sands.
Tears glow on the face of space
Comforting night lights for the human race.

Sleep well, safe, secure, peaceful.
Soundly deeply.
Dream away haunting, daunting, thoughts,
Floating forget-me-nots.
Today drifts away into a long, misty past.
'Goodnight my children' her warm dark blanket
Surrounds all of us.

Julia Kerr

149

A Musical Reflection

Relaxing is a luxury,
Don't often get the chance
But when I do my thoughts stray on,
My mind's eye to enhance.

I seem to hear the mighty sound
Of music from the 'Proms,'
When all our hearts are lifted
By singers and their songs.

We sing of hope and glory
From 'Pomp and Circumstance'
With Elgar's stirring music
We wave our flags and dance.

We feel that we are comrades all
Inspired to sway together
With joyfulness and rapture
And never mind the weather!

The people cheer, conductor smiles
He wipes his brow and waits.
His is the power to 'raise the roof'
To Heaven's golden gates.

Why can't we be united so
At home, at work, at play,
Good neighbours to our fellow men
So Peace will come to stay?

Enid Hewitt

Enchanted Country

I know a land so very beautiful
Almost too lovely to describe
I have been there many, many times
But each is still enchanting
As if I'd never been before
And then it calls me back once more.

Oh land of purple heather
And cheerful winding rivers
I adore your lofty mountains
And valleys down below
Your lakes and glens are unsurpassed
I know I have to go.

The captivating white-washed crafts
Are lovely to behold
With peat fires burning brightly
And hay stacked in the lofts
I am spellbound once again
And overcome with awe.

When I get that strong desire
I must go to that enchanted land
A land of song and music
With a beauty all its own
An inner peace surrounds me
I am in Scotland once again.

Georgina Johnston

Hope

Hope is racing from my fingers and with it the smell of sweet
perfume,
I've lost my chance to start all over,
I've lost the chance to be a groom.
I'm all alone here in the forest, all the birds have flown away,
I knew I should have clinged to Hope,
Can love be found another way?

No longer alone in the forest, a bearded man is on my trail,
He wants to talk for no apparent reason,
I think it's time I should set sail . . .

I'm darting through this blackened fortress,
As I run I shed a tear,
The police pack dogs are in the forest and tracing my smell,
My smell of fear.

I'm bleeding rapidly in this forest, a sergeant's gun looms
Over me,
I'm fading fast, now in this forest,
I'm pretty sure to some degree.

Lying quietly in this forest, it is time to meet my maker,
Though when I'm gone they'll search this forest,
Discover Hope, and then will wake her.

Craig Brown

152

DNA

A pen that writes in every direction
Tracing the story of our lives
Weaving back and forth
Intertwining the years
Linking people and lands
Drawing us back together again
Back to our shared story.

Stella Koenick

Definitions

If you thought you had lost your tomorrow
Or thought that you'd been deceived
Would you think that your life was fruitless?
Or had blossomed with what you achieved.

Our hope for tomorrow defines us
It keeps your mind strong with your soul
To give up your hope for tomorrow
Would be surely to lose your control.

You will see in the light of yesterday
That you cannot change or alter what's past
Instead you must look for tomorrow
And have hope in what you have asked.

And when tomorrow slips over your life
And another is sure to follow
Are you content to look for the next one?
Or are you sad that today was so hollow.

Each day that you lose in your lifetime
Will not be returned to repaid
Instead it is lost forever
As if your whole life was mislaid.

And when you lie dying on your day
Will you think of what could have been?
Or will you just lie there happily content
At what you have learned and have seen.

David Long

Reflections

I remember, I remember the place where I was born
The tree clad hills, lush green fields and rolling fields of corn
The river flowing through the Vale - onward to the sea
Walking through the leafy lanes, my sister, friends and me
Skipping, hoops and hopscotch, were our favourite games
Every day was joyous - not one of them the same
We walked safely through the woods picking daffodils,
Bluebells, many kinds of flowers growing on the hills
The innocence of childhood was ours to enjoy
Without a care to worry us whether girl or boy,
We had imagination - we were warriors and kings,
Next day we'd be cowboys and many other things,
Halcyon days in many ways hold sweet memories yet
We all grew up apace with little to regret -
But - war came and we went to serve in many different fields
Our innocence soon left us and faith became our shield
We hoped and prayed every day the wretched war would end
Months dragged into years and we made other friends
Now we are old, few are left to share the memories
Life is very precious whatever age you'd be.

Myrtle Wright

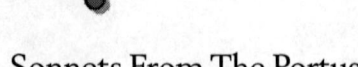

Sonnets From The Portuguese

XLIII

How do I love thee? Let me count the ways.
I love thee to the depth and breadth and height
My soul can reach, when feeling out of sight
For the ends of Being and ideal Grace.
I love thee to the level of everyday's
Most quiet need, by sun and candlelight.
I love thee freely, as men strive for Right;
I love thee purely, as they turn from Praise.
I love thee with the passion put to use
In my old griefs, and with my childhood's faith.
I love thee with a love I seemed to lose
With my lost saints - I love thee with the breath,
Smiles, tears, of all my life! and, if God choose,
I shall but love thee better after death.

Elizabeth Barrett Browning

Love

Through the hardship and pain one thing remains,
so incomprehensible yet perfectly simple,
love.
Day by day strengthening, not once faltering
questioned so often yet never seemed to be doubted.
An absence of longing, of pain,
the heart satisfied with such attachment
trembles passionately with devotion.
Tested through every danger,
true love proven.
The eyes of the heart opened, the bearer clearly sees
all that is to be seen, the world at its best.
All that was dull suddenly brilliant with colour,
all that was lifeless overflowing with life,
all that meant nothing means the world.
The true colours of love found once a lifetime
to be honoured and treasured throughout
all your days.

Lucy Conway

Eternal Flame

Step one, strike a match of mutual attraction,
Ignite with the paper of touch;
Step two, lay on kindling to spark a reaction,
Add love coal with care, not too much,
Or you'll smother the flames, and prevent them from spreading;
Allow them to slowly take hold;
Let them dance to your tune, to ensure the right heading,
For a glow that will never turn cold.
With regular refuelling, in similar fashion,
Not even a dowsing of tears
Will extinguish this fierce conflagration of passion;
May it burn on for millions of years.

Ann P Howes

The Sky

The sky is vast encompassing all
It makes us seem microscopically small
Puffs of fluffy cloud, nonchalantly blowing
Lazily to their destiny are flowing
From the sunset splashes of colour spread,
Mauves, blues, oranges, yellow and red.
Like a moving picture a great master has created.
In oils and water colours, clouds appearing silver plated.

Sky, oh what secrets do you encumber?
Whilst us mortals do deeply slumber.
Have you seen everything we desire to know?
As the days and nights come and go.
Sky you are so mighty and vast,
Forever there overseeing our future present and past.

Polly Glenville

Over The Bridge Beyond The Sea

Over the bridge, beyond the sea,
There is a place where I want to be,
A place where no one has been before,
A place where no one has seen, for,
The sun is always shining, everyone's happy,
There is no war or hatred, the world lives peacefully.
No one gets angry and no one ever cries,
Or if they do, it's tears of joy flowing from their eyes.
Animals live freely, all the people are so gay,
Every moment of their lives is a bright, new, happy day.
All four seasons flowers bloom, so colourful and bold,
Because of all the love and peace this world is never cold.
But none of this is real, it's just a fantasy,
Although there is love and peace there also happens to be,
War and cold hearts, people unhappy,
But gratefully none of this does relate to me.
I live in a lovely world, where everything is great,
To me, my life is perfect, some might call it fate.

Lily Rose White (12)

The Poet

Poetry is the thoughts that we try to analyse,
But poetry is beyond that term it's the thought that begs disguise
It's wrapped up in golden metaphors
To try to give us thought of what it's like to live within
The mind of a thinking poet.

He who speaks in riddles, He who makes us wonder
Does he do it on purpose or does he want us to ponder
To think of things less mundane
Than the dreary round of life
For there is another life we lead
That is in our head
We travel the world far and wide yet
Never stir a foot,
Mountains to climb, rivers to cross
Dragons to fight to boot
Our inner world's a fantasy but
At least it is our own
No one can take it from us, it's
Our castle, our palace, our home.
So what's so strange about poetry
It's another form of dreaming
With words that paint you pictures
Words to set you wondering
Words can stimulate your brain
More powerful than the sword
For in the hands of the gifted one
A word is not just a word!

It's to make you think that in yourself,
There dwells another you, one who
Travels within your mind
To give you another point of view
Of life within as well as without
Life really can be sweet, for
Release the visions stored within,
Who knows, you've found
A poet!

161

R Bateman

Friendship

True friendship is an unbreakable link
she is always there to pull you back from the brink.

Ups and downs there will always be
But if you're feeling down she'll make you happy.

Whatever life throws at your feet
She will help, but she'll always be discreet.

A friend will always help no matter what
She will help you cope with all she's got.

Sometimes you won't agree with the advice you receive
But it is always given with her heart on her sleeve.

When you are feeling unhappy she will give you a lift
Yes, true friendship is a remarkable gift.

Cindy Roberts

Smile!

It's said a smile is priceless
The only thing in life that's free,
Bringing joy and happiness
No one can disagree!

It makes a beggar in the street
The luckiest man alive,
A millionaire is poor without one,
A smile you just cannot buy.

It costs nothing to give one,
It means the world to receive,
Cheering up unhappy people
Making those without faith believe.

So give a little something
Cheer up someone by miles,
Nothing is greater
Than receiving a smile!

Chloe Sweeney (14)

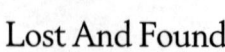

Lost And Found

So loving and giving a lovely caring man.
Everything was achievable once it was began
Life so charmed, it could only be wished for.
Careless actions sadly meant happiness was no more.
Sweet life declined and disappeared, it all seemed so unfair.
Reality bit deep within your soul, did you really care?
Doubt and self pity overtook your gracious life.
Hell bent on destruction, you carried on among strife.
All alone time to sit and ponder.
Surrounded by strangers, sadly no friends any longer.
Left alone on an island of sorrows and lies.
Was it really the so called friends, who planned your demise.
New hope as reality dawns, your goodness will shine
through.
Storm clouds passing, sun blazing in a sky of blue.
Repairing the hurt is a long lonely road.
Accepting you were wrong will lighten the load.
Happiness will soon be yours
Now you have discovered, we all have flaws.
Life sadly will never be the same.
Circumstances occur, don't look for someone to blame.
Learn by life's ups and downs.
You are so much richer, not necessarily by pounds.
Your new found belief makes you stronger from within.
Go forward with hope, as your new life does begin.

Anne Sackey

Shoes

I travelled far in many years,
Complaining of no shoes,

Until the day I met a man:
A simpler life he'd choose,

His memory I will honour,
As now I am complete,

When I complained I had no shoes,
I found he had no feet.

David Thomas

Restored

And love brings peace - where turmoil rules.
It stays and grows
Not fail, or abuse.
Fix the injured, poor in soul
Turn the damaged into whole.

T Lawrence

Problems

Don't talk about your problems anymore
Don't water them anymore,
Just let them become dry,
Let them wither and die,

For talking is watering,
And watering is growing.
Don't talk about your problem anymore,
Just let them wither and die,
Just let them wither and die,
Just let them wither and die.

S Booth

Untitled

You give me the courage to stand up and fight
To not give in when I know I'm right.
If faced with a challenge I wouldn't even try
When pushed too far, I'd just break down and cry.
You give me the courage to believe in myself
To push myself forward, not sit on the shelf
If the crowd went one way, then I used to follow
Hide what I wanted, conceal my sorrow
You give me the courage to share my dreams
To reveal what's inside, my plans, my schemes
I appeared too shallow, 'cold as ice'
Afraid of rejection, I'd always think twice
You give me the courage to live every day
To reach my potential, you showed me the way.

Alyson Belcher

Roller Coaster

I've ridden the roller coaster
The past eight months gone,
It's been a bumpy ride -
Up and down all along.

Now I want to settle
On more stable ground,
So my life will stop spinning
Around and around.

God reached down and invited me
To take His hand.
He persisted, so I took it,
And found more level ground.

He's loosened His grip
So I may run and be free,
But whenever I fall down,
He'll be there for me.

I have to trust in His promise
And believe in His word.
Whenever he does reach down,
My prayer for help He's heard.

I want to live like a child,
So happy and free,
Knowing full well
He's taking care of me.

It doesn't take much -
Faith like a mustard seed,
And the will to do His will,
As He lives in me.

Julie Sennitt

169

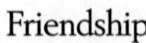

Friendship

In memory, I can walk
The forest glade with you,
Like brothers, step by step;
And feel the warmth of the sun
Glimmering through a canopy of green,
Hearing the unseen sounds;
A place for dreams to be made;
In all of this our voices mingle;
We talk of many things,
Of the past, then today's events,
And of the unknowing future:
We walk the forest path
Just as passing light in time:
Our understanding and friendship
Will stay firm like the mountains
Where eagles soar in majestic flight;
And distance is no barrier in all of this.

Nine Mirasol

If Only

As time goes by and days drift on
And people wonder why,
They never give a thought for
Things or even glance an eye.
They never give much time for
Life in their dark and shabby rooms,
With cold damp walls that hold all dreams,
And lives that slip away.
If only people took the time
An hour in one day, to look around
At things they have which never go away.

Kathleen Graham

A Day?

Each day is a challenge,
Each day creates goals,
Each day hurdles surface,
Each day obstacles arise,
Each day criticism is thrown,
Each day hearts take beating,
Each day souls lose depth,
Each day dies.

Each day sunrise, sun falls,
Each day moon shines and calls,
Each day life dies,
Each day life is born,
Each day wars, erupt, crime increases,
Each day the world ticks, ticks on,
Each and every day,
Babies are born,
The sun shines,
Medicines save, miracles happen.

Each and every day,
Great words are spoken,
Life and nature grows,
Each and every day,
I live as if it were my last,
Each and every day,
Are our present and our past?

Suzanne Tattersall

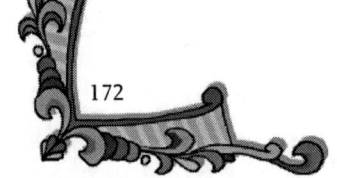

Puppy Love

Gently, she lays her head on my knee.
Then, two luminous orbs start to hypnotise me.
The time for her walk has come round again,
And a mesmeric message burns into my brain.

Lay down your paper, get up from that chair;
Now go to the door, my lead's hanging there.
Put on your coat, and lace up your shoes,
Oh, why can't you hurry, there's no time to lose.

This little charade we play twice a day;
I cannot resist, like a slave I obey.
I fumble with zips, and tussle with ties,
Watched all the time by two button bright eyes.

Out in the fields, she'll pause at a stile,
And I'll watch as she sniffs at the air for a while.
I muse as she chooses the route for our walk.
Who was it that said: Animals can't talk?

David Walker

Love Lives On

Today I wake in a wash of fresh memories,
For last night I met with my love once again;
We danced for happy times past,
With eyes locked, bodies close and tight;
Yet with the morning sun his soul has taken flight,
So I wish that I may dream again tonight.

Cherished are the days when he filled my life,
Holding me through winter's chill, beside me in summer's
gold;
Sharing a love as deep as the ocean,
With hearts that rode through life,
On sweet waves of unity.

A tear is shed for those days now past,
When he basked in my joy and befriended my fear;
Yet shine he does as a star in heaven,
Showering his love from up above,
Upon my hungry heart.

So my love has not left me in his flight,
No, he waits to greet me in dreams of the night.

Samantha Zachariah

God Is Love

Gather all your thoughts together,
  Put them in a prayer,
    Go your way with heart rejoicing,
      God is everywhere!

Never dwell on yesterday,
  Think only of tomorrow,
    But, from the past, learn lessons wisely,
      If they be joy - or sorrow.

Do each task a little better
  and spread the warmth of love,
    Your day's will so much brighter be
      and you'll know that God - is love!

Maggie Cartridge

Quintessence

There are splendid sunsets I shall never see,
and roses that will bloom beyond my sight;
Yet have I seen of all earth's loveliness
the essence, since you filled my days with light.

There are songs that never will enchant mine ears,
and birds that sing in spheres beyond my reach;
yet all the richest harmonies of heaven
resound for me in your harmonious speech.

There are joys and hopes that I shall never know,
and sorrows that forbear to shed my tears;
yet all the wrack and ecstasy of life
you brought to me, and all the shining years.

R Probert

God-Given Peace

I sat upon a craggy height,
My head down my knees.
A conflict raged within my heart,
My mind was ill at ease.

I'd come to seek the peace of God,
But where could it be found?
For even here, alone, I heard
Earth's noises all around.

I heard the whirring of the looms
In textile mills below;
I heard the traffic on the road,
The river's rushing flow.

I looked up, and saw clouds roll past,
The sky no longer blue,
But, like my thoughts, grey, overcast;
The sun had vanished too.

Yet, as I sat, God gave me peace,
Peace that made every part
Of life into a harmony -
His peace, deep in my heart!

Nancy Solly

Within Our Heart

H ope that I can be, of aid,
A nd what, we say, can help, instead,
V ery soon, our minds, make clear,
E very heart, must not, know fear,

I 've said it long, oft, many times,

T he task, be hard, the hills, to climb,
H eal division, when we can,
E ngage our minds, have hope, of plan,

T error has been, no sense, of while,
I njuries many, a hope conceal,
M any a family, are torn, in two,
E ach every one, their life, ensue,

T hink hard, thy thoughts,
O f have, no costs,

A nd say, that I, can be, a friend
N o to strife, I shall intend,
S hall we now, sit down, to say,
W e will help, our love convey,
E very time, there is, depress,
R eply and say, I want no less,

T urn away, from what, is wrong,
O pen your heart, say I belong,

Y ou have my word, I want, no more,
O urselves alone, we will deplore,
U se our strength, to help renew,
R eclaim our lives, we can, so too,

C alm our part, within our fears,
A im to capture, all lost tears
L et's be strong, we can agree,
L earn to love, our hopeful plea.

Hugh Campbell

June 13th

Be Thankful

When you awake at the start of the day
Spare a thought along the way
For those whose lives are touched by sadness
For those that have
And others much less
For those with illness
And those that have lost
For those in wars
And those in famine
Spare a thought as you begin each morning
And thank God.
A great new day is dawning.

Elizabeth Hall

A Dream Place

Somewhere quiet to sit;
Maybe beside the wall
Where the sun shines
On the bricks and a chair
Is there to give me rest.
With warmth on my face
And sunshine on the flowers.

My own special place
A bamboo chair on the patio
With flowered chintz covers,
To lift my spirits up.
Somewhere I can remember
And feel it to be true -
The sunshine and the flowers.

Or am I just recalling,
The sunlit days of youth?

Janet Lamport

Believe What You See

Don't believe all you hear
Believe what you see
Seeing is believing
Surmised gossip can cost dear.

Surmising can make one into a liar
It is harmful and causes distress
By all means gossip if needs be
If only the truth you speak.

Don't believe all you hear
From spiteful tongues,
Listen to happy news
About those you hold dear.

Those with bitter tongues
Are not happy people,
They judge others by themselves
And know not right from wrong.

So be happy in your mind
Believing things are not always what they seem to be,
Look for the good and you will find
Others will follow in your style.

Hetty Foster

Dad

Blackbird singing early morning,
Goldfinches stopping on their way.
Cuckoo comes without warning.
Maybe a swallow you will see
When you come to visit me.
I shall take comfort
In all of these things,
I'll not be sad,
When I think of *Dad*.

The scent of new-mown hay,
Muck spreading on an autumn day.
Horses running in the fields,
Maybe a butterfly you will see
When you come to visit me.
I shall take comfort
In all of these things,
I'll not be sad,
When I think of *Dad*.

Time has passed.
Good memories stay.
It couldn't be any other way.
He loved the country
And all that it means.
Maybe a teardrop you will see
When you come to visit me.
I shall take comfort
In all of these things
I'll not be sad,
When I think of *Dad*.

S Draper

Star Chaser

Star gazer, moon chaser
Flying through the wind
Asking questions
Seeking answers
Forgiveness for your sins

Chase the wind, seek the sun
Fly free amongst the clouds
Forget the answers
And the questions
Just learn to stand proud

The stars won't tell
The moon is silent
No whispers on the wind
Look within for the answers
Forget about your sins

Sins are part of living
Self forgiveness is the key
So chasing the moon
And asking the stars
Are not where you must seek

Forgive yourself
And watch the world
The sun, the moon, the stars
Dance with the words upon the wind
Then let your soul fly far.

Alison Colley

Life's Reward

Such fun for thee
To rise in the morn
Filled with glee
And not be forlorn

One feels uplifted
To accepting what comes
Feeling contented
When work is done

Whatever the weather
To happily go thou forward
Overlooking all tether
Life has its reward

To make thy days pleasant
Assists other folk too
Filling them with sentiment
If only a few

Realising the mind
Is as a clock,
Keeping it wind
It doth not get blocked

Life can be made a joy
Not just going out and about
And without feeling coy
Home is good without doubt.

Josephine Foreman

Unique

Presence so intense,
Everything so real,
Reflect on the past
Focus on the future.
Ending loneliness,
Creating happiness.
True and real,
Laughter and fun,
Occurred randomly -
Vibrantly full.
Everything to me.

Katrina Maconaghie

A Silent Friend

Have you ever felt the shivers
Icy fingers down your spine?
Have you ever known the presence
In dark stairways as you climb
When you walk the hours of darkness?
Have you felt you're not alone
Felt the silent ghostly wanderer
Walking with you as you roam?
Have you ever walked with spirits
Misted visions on the stairs
Felt the chilling of the blood
The prickling of the neck with rising hairs?
Have you ever sat dreamy in the flickering fire glow,
Massaged by uneasy feelings by hands that never show,
Felt the tugging of your clothes or maybe the gentle shove,
Heard the creaking of silent floorboards from empty
                                    bedrooms up above?
If you have you've spent an evening hosted by a departed
                                    friend you love.

B Wardle

A Prayer To Begin The Day

Oh Lord! Please help me carefully through this working day,
Give me the health, the strength, the courage, the wisdom,
The knowledge, the insight, the foresight, the intelligence,
The heroism, and the bravery,
Whatever it takes to help me carefully through this day,
And bring me to its close with peace of mind.

Martin J Harvey

Spirit Of The World

The wonders of the universe,
the many joys and pleasures in life.
First found by young sweethearts,
though sometimes sadly lost later, by trouble war and strife.

The beauty of a mild sweet heady fresh spring day,
when the loveliness of each flower can take your breath
away.

The miracle of birth, and the sadness of death,
when we alas draw, our very last breath.
But all is not lost, for our souls will still live on,
and our spirit will still remain and never truly be gone.

For when the world was created, it was never meant to die.
So remember this, when you next look up to the sky.

Deanne Southgate

Lawrence's Four-Footed Friends

My grandson Lawrence is rather like me;
In animal matters we both agree.
With his arm gently encircling Sweep,
He calls out 'Grandma, come quickly, peep.'

Because I can read him like a book,
Whatever I'm doing, I leave to look.
I know very well what needs to be done,
Another picture with two entwined as one.

I grab the camera to prepare for the shot.
You wouldn't believe the number I've got.
There's Lawrence with Misty and with Tara too,
With Scamper and Kerry; any will do.

Each of these is, or has been, our dog or cat,
But they're his as well - his devotion deserves that.
It's just the same with those we meet outside;
He smiles, bending down, with his arms open wide.

He relates to them all and my heart glows with joy
At the mutual affection between animal and boy.
I'm optimistic that, as the years do enfold,
He'll always have animals to love and to hold.

Ina J Harrington

On Reflection

My mind is blank
Like the paper before me
But yet, these words appear
Now as I look, what do I see?
We need to hold on to the past,
To make us strong
To ensure the future,
Find out where we belong.
What happened yesterday,
Will live in our minds forever
Insanity let loose
Do we submit, no never!
Forces of evil we deny,
The path of righteousness is narrow
Follow with care,
Beware the poisoned arrow.
History is full of fanatics
Each day we live, becomes the past
Monsters live amongst us
The die is cast!
To live together.
Colour, creed or race
The future of this world
Not outer space!
For this must be the dream
Of each and everyone,
To live in peace, give thanks
Each day, beneath the setting sun!

T G Bloodworth
September 12th 2001

190

You

If you were given a blank sheet to draw up a new life
Would you omit all your sorrows, your troubles, your strife?
Would you leave out the difficult people you've met
And those who believe that you are a threat?
Would you be healthy, wealthy and wise?
But then how would you know this - let's just surmise
Our experience provides insight, we can feel at first hand
What it's like to be that person in a particular land
If nobody hurt us, how would we learn to forgive?
If it wasn't for dying, would we know how to live?
If there wasn't positive and negative in everything
Then we could not choose to do the right thing
If your path in life has gone sadly a-wry
And you are forever asking oh God why
You must have chosen to live it this way
But there are other factors that will brighten your day
It could be a rainbow, it could be a smile
There are positive things going on all the while
They will lighten your spirit, they will help you renew
For the most important person in your life is *you*!

brightlaurastar

Sometimes . . .

(Dedicated To My Friend)

Sometimes when faced with a crisis
When unsure of the right path to take
When afraid to make a decision
So afraid to make a mistake
When lost in a Sea of Confusion
Adrift on a Tide of Despair
When the world is crashing around you
Then reach out, and you'll find me there
Sometimes we need someone to talk to
Or maybe just be close at hand
A shoulder you know you can lean on
Not to judge, but just understand
For often the answer you're seeking
Will all become clear in the end
Just believe in your own inner conscience
And the help and support of a friend.

Stephanie M Bines

Luke 15: 1 - 32 - Prodigal Son

11. And he said, A certain man has two sons:
12. And the younger of them said to his father, Father, give me the portion of good that falleth to me. And he divided unto them his living.
13. And not many days after the younger son gathered all together, and took his journey into a far country, and there wasted his substance with riotous living.
14. And when he had spent all, there arose a mighty famine in that land; and he began to be in want.
15. And he went and joined himself to a citizen of that country; and he sent him into the fields to feed swine.
16. And he would fain have filled his belly with the husks that the swine did eat: and no man gave unto him.
17. And when he came to himself, he said, How many fired servants of my father's have bread enough and to spare, and I perish with hunger!
18. I will arise and go to my father, and will say unto him, Father, I have sinned against heave, and before thee,
19. And am no more worthy to be called thy son: make me as one of thy hired servants.
20. And he arose, and came to his father. But when he was yet a great way off, his father saw him, and had compassion, and ran, and fell on his neck, and kissed him.
21. And the son said unto him, Father, I have sinned against heaven, and in thy sight, and no more worthy to be called thy son.
22. But the father said to his servants, Bring forth the best robe, and put it to him; and put a ring on his hand, and shoes on his feet:
23. And bring hither the fatted calf, and kill it; and let us eat, and be merry:
24. For this my son was dead, and I alive again; he was lost, and is found. And they began to be merry.

Perfect Day

As I look out of my window, I ponder,
My thoughts they drift as I often wonder.
The light is going, its heavenly way,
As this is the end of a beautiful day.

A perfect day as I could ever hope,
A perfect blue sky, full of scope.
And now as the sun seeks its rest,
This is the time it looks its best.

The sky so clear, and so deep blue,
The horizon filled with a crimson hue.
The time plays its game, with the night,
And the colours mellow within our sight.

The birds recognise the day is past,
The light gets dim, and vanishes fast.
The blue turns darker, and blends as one,
As we wait again for the rise of the sun.

Dawn Graham

The Gospel According To St Mark (Chapter 6 - Loaves And Fishes)

34. And Jesus, when he came out, saw much people, and was moved with compassion toward them, because they were as sheep not having a shepherd: and he began to teach them many things.

35. And when the day was now far spent, his disciples came unto him, and said, This is a desert place, and now the time is far passed:

36. Send them away, that they may go into the country round about, and into the villages, and buy themselves bread: for they have nothing to eat.

37. He answered and said unto them, Give ye them to eat. And they say unto him, Shall we go and buy two hundred pennyworth of bread, and give them to eat.

38. He saith unto them, How many loaves have ye? go and see. And when they knew, they say, Five, and two fishes.

39. And he commanded them to make all sit down by companies upon the green grass.

40. And they sat down in ranks, by hundreds, and by fifties.

41. And when he had taken the five loaves and the two fishes, he looked up to heaven, and blessed, and brake the loaves, and gave them to his disciplines to set before them; and the two fishes divided he among them all.

42. And they did all eat, and were filled.

43. And they took up twelve baskets full of the fragments, and of the fishes.

44. And they that did eat of the loaves were about five thousand men.

Ode To The Angels

Beautiful beings
of heavenly light
ethereal angels
loving and kind,

guiding and supporting
on life's long journey.
Invisible, unseen you may be
yet I know you are here.

Protective and compassionate
you always hover near.
Your presence enfolds me
in golden light all
through this precious life.

Thank you, thank you
lovely beings of light.
Thank you for your
love and concern.

And thank you
all the angels
who still live on this earth,

whose helping hand
and loving care
I could not do without.

Love is all
Love is light.
Without love
there is only
Eternal night.

Brigitta D'Arcy

Thinking Time

From morn to night many chores are done.
Cleaning and cooking is not much fun.
It is important to have thinking time.
Some quiet moments to compose a rhyme.
Stop jobs when a friend calls for a chat,
Conversation with information about this or that.
It's good to talk about one's problems and cares.
Usually one's visitor gets talking about theirs.
Does one good to have advice and consolation.
More of this, we'd be a healthy nation.

Ann May Wallace

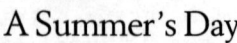

A Summer's Day

Nice weather, it's really warm,
Bees are out and in a swarm.
Drink in one hand, ice cream in other,
Coke's all gone, I'll get another.
I have never felt so good,
I don't think I ever would.
The sun is shining, I feel happy,
Never again will I be snappy.
But clouds come out and hide the sun,
No more sunshine, no more fun.
Maybe tomorrow it'll be hot,
But knowing our weather maybe not.

Gabrielle Ann Conway (12)

The Homecoming

In the far distance, a bell is ringing,
nearer to home young carollers are singing
The freezing cold wind blows sleet in my face
I blow on my hands and quicken my pace,
head down, collar up this bleak winter night,
turning the corner, there's a welcome light,
chilled to the bone feeling numb and raw,
a scarlet holly wreath hangs on my door.

Warmth surrounds me as stumbling into the light
I close the door on the dark freezing night,
hustle and bustle meets my tired eyes
out of the oven comes hot mince pies
everyone greets me with joyful hugs and kisses.
Come, stir the pudding and make your wishes
bringing the Christmas tree is traditionally mine
smells of spice and oranges mingle with pine.

With my back to the fire, my body glows,
as feeling comes back to fingers and toes.
All peace in the house, no squabbles or fights,
Grandad, still trying to untangle the lights,
feeling contented with a glass of mulled wine
sitting and gazing at this family of mine.

Moon Stone

Things Can't Be That Bad!

Even when skies
Are cloudy.
Despite cold wind and rain
There's a sun
That can shine
Inside of us,
So look in the mirror
And *smile*!

Lyn Sandford

Our Wedding Day

On a hot sunny day those words we did say,
Till death us do part, you're always in my heart.
That short day in July, I remember my mother's cry,
The tears of joy and sadness all rolled into one,
My anxious feelings reassured by the sight of the sun.
The shining beautiful wedding car,
That didn't need to travel far.
The happy smiling faces of people young and old,
I wonder if it would have been the same, if it had been cold.
All my friends and family together in one place,
Gazing around in happiness, not one unhappy face.
A day to remember and to treasure,
Such happiness we feel and so much pleasure.
Guests dressed up smart in hats and suits,
The pageboy running around looking ever so cute.
The cake being cut and the cameras flash,
The rest just before the evening bash.
The day that flew by ever so fast,
But the memories remain and will always last.

Helen Rees-Smith

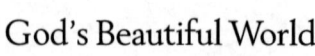

God's Beautiful World

I love God's beautiful world,
The sunshine on the lake,
The towering mountains
So strong and protective,
The stillness of the shady woods,
The wild flowers along the lane.
They all boast unashamedly
of God's glory.
Rivers and streams speak
of his overflowing love.
The birds sing out his praises.
They have no problem
in accepting God's goodness and love.
They live for today,
not knowing what tomorrow will bring.
Father God
I too am part of your creation.
Help me to accept your goodness and love,
to live for today,
and to believe that I too
am as precious to you
as your beautiful world.

Maggie Reid

The Sower

'Not what you say, but what you are.'
These were the wise words spoken.
They remain true in every age
where promises are broken.
Knowledge withers as years pass by,
Overburdened by all that is known:
Yet, what you have lived every day of your life,
experienced through joy or the pain of strife,
is your harvest from what you have sown.

Diana Morcom

Give A Thought

What would we do without carers,
And by now I have met quite a few,
Looking after the sick and elderly.
As the families could not do.

All those in care are different,
Their wants change from day to day,
So trying to keep them contented,
Your feelings, must be put away.

A mood or a tantrum could be part of their day,
But these you must take in your stride,
You know it is not really them,
It's just they have nowhere to hide.

A smile or a chat could be your reward,
They know that you really care,
And will often do their very best,
To lighten the load that you bear.

Those little acts of kindness,
Carried out so willingly,
Shows the caring spirit,
That others do not see.

So just give a thought for those,
Who use their time and skill,
Looking after the sick and elderly,
And the service they fulfil.

Will A Tilyard

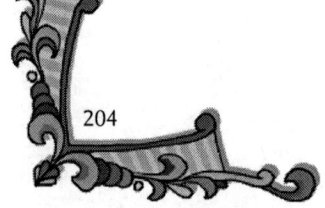

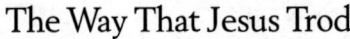

The Way That Jesus Trod

To have lived in the days of Jesus
Would be my one delight
To tread the steps my saviour trod
And pray with him all night.

To see the lowly stable where
Wise men came to see
The young Mary and Joseph
With baby Jesus on their knee.

To see him with the fishermen
Peter, James and John
All the faithful being healed
Whom Jesus put hands on.

The lady who touched his hem
And the woman at the well
The blind man at the gate
And sinners saved from hell.

And yet it's such a privilege
To have heard but never seen
For a faithful heart is sure to have
Special blessings from the king.

Sonia Riggs

Hold On To Love

Love can be forever
Or a passing in the night
It can glow and shimmer
With translucent light.

It is in a heartbeat
Or in a gentle smile
In a passionate embrace
Or just being close for a while.

Love is a splendid emotion
On which to build your life
It will help you carry on
Through life's struggle and strife.

If you have love, hold onto it
Never let go
For without it life is not the same
As you may already know.

So if your heart says keep trying
Though your head says no
You have the right to feel happy
If you don't it's time to let go.

Jeanette Jackson

The Butterfly

Brief is the life of a butterfly,
Flitting from flower to flower,
Savouring the heady nectar
Secretly within.

Its beauty gives such pleasure
To all who watch it pass:
The vivid colours of its wings
Reflecting summer sun.

However long or short our lives,
Let each and every moment
Bring fulfilment to our hearts:
No wasted time.

May others see in us,
Something that brings them hope,
Pleasure and comfort in their lives,
Like beauteous butterfly.

Roma Davies

Write About Me

I see you write about me
To make up a poem or a song
Am I such a hurtful soul
That all your love for me has gone.

I see you write about me
In the middle of the night
For you say you find it hard to sleep
While I can sleep so tight.

I see you write about me
Even as I leave
But you cannot write about
The things I do not let you see.

Keith Powell

Children Of The Future

Children of the future,
World peace is in your hands.
Carve your way through life like a sculptor,
And give the love the world demands.

Be elegant and graceful,
In everything you should do.
A world so very peaceful,
And children it all depends on you.

Remember that truth and honesty,
Shall always prevail.
Above all the fear and hatred,
And particularly blackmail.

So children lead the way,
To a better fulfilled life.
But remember every day,
This has to work world-wide.

Christopher Roberts

Since Love Came . . .

Now love has come into my life
It lifts my soul
Makes me whole . . .

Now love has come into my life
It is only meet
That I am complete . . .

For so long, I was drowning in the mire
Now that I have found you, you inspire
Me to see each morning the golden lantern that lights up the sky
And I would gladly give my life for you, for you I would gladly die.

You fill up my senses, as the rose bursts into bloom
You bestow a blessing, as the flowers perfume
I would rather walk on broken glass,
Than see a teardrop form in your eye
I would rather break my heart in two,
Then give my half to you, than you cry
For you are my star that shines so bright
My guide in the deepest, darkest, night.

For you are my love
And there is no other
You bring music to my soul
Till my dying day
You are my all, my whole
Life! Let's love, I pray
Till the rhythm of our hearts cease
And we fly h'venward in peace . . .

Mary A Shovlin

210

Beatitudes Of The Blind

Blessed are those whose arm I can take
In strange surroundings in walks we make.

Blessed are those who wait for a while
Giving me time to cross that tall stile.

Blessed are they who clasp my hand
And share the problems I can't understand.

Blessed are they who are happy to wait
Till I put down my cup, before taking my plate.

Blessed are they who know I would wish
To finish the meal if I locate the dish.

Blessed are those who realise why
I feel if the chair is low or high.

Blessed are those who tell me about
The things all around when I can't go out.

Blessed are those who just love me,
Ignoring the fact that I cannot see.

Margaret Connolly

Reality

Too much reality
day by day
does you no good
there is need for more play
a chance to explore those woods
come out of the trees
stop and look
smell the breeze
feel the difference
all of its own
the chance to roam, all alone
embrace a little time
so precious and complete
reality can wait
so dip a toe in
then paddle the feet.

Katherine Parker

Moving House

When the house you have dreamed of at last has come true
the sale is agreed and formalities gone through.
Excitement is mounting as moving draws near,
there are boxes to pack and cupboards to clear.
Carpets to choose, and curtains to measure,
items to sort that we care for and treasure.

This house so familiar, is quiet and bare,
now that the family are no longer there.
No laughter is heard, from children at play,
or the fights and the squabbles that were part of the day.
No more need of that love that soothed many a tear,
or the Mum that remembers these memories so dear.

Just the two of us now, with a new life ahead,
to furnish with love, as the last path we tread.
Opportunities beckon, thoughts of freedom seem sweet
with a small comfy house, to keep tidy and neat.
As the chaos around me gets worse, I declare,
I wish I could wake up, and find myself there.

Margaret Wilson

213

Faith Reborn

I had drifted away though I loved You still
In my vague uncaring way
With plenty to do and so much in view
That I seldom found time to pray

Then the years all crept on and retirement came
Giving lots of time to spare
With Alpha about though still full of doubt
Curiosity took me there

With a feeling of 'I've heard all this before'
From my friends in days gone by
As life hurried on my interest was gone
And I needed to find out why

In a night when the air was all filled with peace
And such calm and sweet content
The time was just right with God in my sight
But my mind in a state unbent.

Then You came unto me and I fought You hard
And I felt 'why bother me?'
My life is quite good, so why ever should
There be need for a talk with Thee.

Then a vision of light startling pure and clear
Just exploded in my mind
So plainly I'd seen how stupid I'd been
To be fighting and oh so blind.

Now I'm walking with You and I talk with You
And I bless the day You came
I want to impart the song in my heart
As I honour Your glorious Name.

Enid Gill

214

No More Will I Roam

No more will I roam from
the place where I was born,
a great deal of water
has passed under the bridge,
now it's time for me to come home.

Many places have I seen,
numerous friends have come my way,
but there is no place like home,
so no more will I roam.

There are times when I forget
the names of people that once I knew,
old age does not come alone,
Yes! It's time to return home.

I recall the time . . . how easily I forget,
if only I could remember where
we met and what we did . . .?
My mind goes blank,
no more will I roam.

Robert Gerald

Why Worry?

Why do we worry about what tomorrow will bring
when we are safely protected beneath His wing?
Why do we worry about what lies ahead
when by His hand we are gently led?

Why do we worry and worry in vain
pondering and seeking the future to gain,
Fretting and fussing about what might be
instead of praying and trusting and waiting to see?

Why by worrying do we spoil our todays,
are we not kept in His love now and always;
closely protected, safe from all harm
embraced and upheld by His loving arms?

So worry not, and do not fret anymore,
God's love for you has opened His store
of blessings, for the morrow new, just
as He has always promised He would do.

Catherine Riley

The Music Of Life

Across the stresses of life
I hear the sounds of my mood in music
It nourishes me, it sustains me
It carries me, it saves me
I see all the days of my life
As the song starts I go back
To the sounds and the places in time
Sometimes happy, sometimes sad
With every beat, with every bar, with every line
This was my spring, this was my summer, and now my autumn
And now my winter approaches
I can find my warmth through my personal music box
The turntable stacked turning and turning inside my head

Les Allen

For Auntie Emmie On Her Birthday

I have a super-duper aunt,
It's true she's far from young,
And as I, myself, am over the hill
Her praises must be sung.
The Queen Mum might be wonderful,
But she has help galore,
Auntie Emmie does it all herself
While still being quite 'top drawer'.
Her house and garden sparkle,
She's just off to 'B&Q'
For paint to brighten her front door
That she alone will do.
So nifty with her needle,
There's nothing she can't sew,
And when she's in the kitchen
Nothing rises like her dough.
She makes style look so simple,
But you've either got it - or you've not,
It's nowt to do with money
But making the most of what you've got.

So let those bubbles dance and fizz
As we raise our glasses once again
To drink to my super-duper aunt
In glorious cool champagne.

Gloria Thorne

218

Art Forms

Is this word defined for the very few?
Not so.
Art can be in all of you.
Whatever shape or form it takes,
Either with chalk, pencils or paint,
To form that picture your mind will create,
Sometimes a doodle,
Not being quite sure,
But after a moment or two,
In thought without having lessons.
Not even being taught.
Just let your imagination run wild
And paint that picture that's there in your mind.
Not caring at all what others may say,
Just carry on painting in your own happy way.
The truest form of art lies deep in the soul,
And just remember when you start
Let your feelings flow
From within your heart.

T Usher

My Life

When life throws hazards my way
I turn and look inside
When nothing is going right
I know I have my pride
When others are hurtful and mean
I smile and do not hide
When the world is on my shoulders
I let me be my guide.

Lindsey Brown

The Colours Of Life

Life, like refraction in panes of coloured glass
Bright times of joy, dark times of sorrow pass
When life is happy, colours gleam and shine
Within life's glass, our thoughts can there entwine
We watch the colours light, and then will find
Peace, deep inside the glass, to soothe our minds
White winter's snow to see on calmer days
Yellow sunshine, buttercups, golden haze
The verdant green of springtime in the trees
Pink blossoms swaying gently in the breeze
Happiness to see in the clear blue sky
Beauty of the sunset to gladden the eye
Orange, red and pink, glowing in twilight
Fading into grey, then to the dark night
Those colours, brightly shining, always there
Some days, we cannot see, through black despair
We may not see, when sorrow dims our eyes
That brightness, there, beneath a dark cloud lies
In sadness, and in loss, our days seem grey
Our troubles make the colours fade away
But soon, when we recover, once again
We'll see through, to the sunshine, from the rain
And there in all their glory, when clouds pass
Life's colours shine on, in those panes of glass

J Jones

The Senses

When alone in solitude and silence,
Has the bustling city hushed its voice,
Does the ticking clock stop?

Daily in our homes,
We cleanse away dust formation,
Yet with limited vision, rarely see the flight,

Fragrance on a woman beguiles the male,
Yet often it is in the garden he lingers,
Is a flower's perfume sweeter?

Taste is a matter of preference,
Culinary masterpieces, or microwave 'quickies'
Where famine exists a grain of rice is sufficient,

Touch between humans and with the animal kingdom,
Results in an emotional exchange,
Does the inanimate object also reciprocate?

How often do we take for granted,
The senses with which we are blessed,

The fortunate are able to listen to musical orchestrations,
Or the conversation of a friend,

See God's wonderful creations in nature,
Stand and admire a mountain, valley or stream,

Delight in the fragrance of a vast array of flowers,
And aromatherapy oils,

Satisfy the palate with appetising food,
Savoury or sweet,

Cradle a newborn baby,
Embrace a loved one, stroke a cat or dog,

Yet there are those who fate decreed,
Would be restricted by sensory loss,
Today let us appreciate these, our special gifts.

Ann G Wallace

Living By Heart

Transcend rationality and you are instantly as free as a child,
able to see with clear eyes, to understand things,
the reasoning mind never could. By this we thrive,
for we are most fully and naturally alive when we live by heart.

Pamela Constantine

Safe In His Arms

God knows all your pain and struggles
God sees all your hidden tears
His love is ever there around you
Calming all your unspoken fears
He will wrap his arms around you
Hold you tight in his care
Meeting all your deepest longings
That you may know he's always there

He will catch you when you stumble
He will never let you fall
Even when you feel forgotten
He will answer your every call
You can trust the love he offers
He will never let you go
For eternity he's promised
That his love for you he'll show.

Sandra Barton

O Tell Me The Truth About Love

Some say that love's a little boy,
And some say it's a bird,
Some say it makes the world go round,
And some say that's absurd,
And when I asked the man next-door,
Who looked as if he knew,
His wife got very cross indeed,
And said it wouldn't do.

Does it look like a pair of pyjamas,
Or the ham in a temperance hotel?
Does its odour remind one of llamas,
Or has it a comforting smell?
Is it prickly to touch as a hedge is,
Or soft as eiderdown fluff?
Is it sharp or quite smooth at the edges?
O tell me the truth about love.

Our history books refer to it
In cryptic little notes,
It's quite a common topic on
The Transatlantic boats;
I've found the subject mentioned in
Accounts of suicides,
And even seen it scribbled on
The backs of railway guides.
Does it howl like a hungry Alsatian,
Or boom like a military band?
Could one give a first rate imitation
On as saw or a Steinway Grand?
Is its singing at parties a riot?
Does it only like classical stuff?

Will it stop when one wants to
be quiet?
O tell me the truth above love.
I looked inside the summer house;
it wasn't ever there:
I tried the Thames at Maidenhead,
And Brighton's bracing air.
I don't know what the blackbird sang,
Or what the tulip said;
But it wasn't in the chicken run,
Or underneath the bed.
Can it pull extraordinary faces?
Is it usually sick on a swing?
Does it spend all its time at the races,
Or fiddling with pieces of string?
Has it views of its own about money?
Does it think patriotism enough?
Are its stories vulgar and funny?
O tell me the truth about love.

When it comes, will it come without
warning
Just as I'm picking my nose?
Will it knock on my door in the morning,
Or tread in the bus on my shoes?
Will it come like a change in the weather?
Will its greeting be courteous or rough?
Will it alter my life altogether?
O tell me the truth about love.

W H Auden

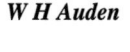

225

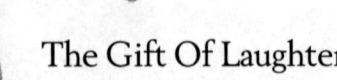

The Gift Of Laughter

Thank you God for the gift of laughter,
The spontaneous response to humour,
The tears of joy welling up in our eyes,
The release of emotion into the air.
Laughter is the best medicine, we are told,
Perhaps if we laughed a bit more
We would do ourselves a favour
And even live a little longer!

For there's a reason to be cheerful
When you're feeling blue,
Just a little inspiration can spark a flame in you . . .
A word of encouragement here and there,
A smile on someone's face,
The kind words of a complete stranger,
A song that touches your heart,
A beautiful painting,
A poem that leaps out of the page,
A Bible verse that speaks to you in a fresh new way.

Where would we be without laughter?
God has coloured our lives with such an amazing gift
To share with one another.

Cathy Mearman

Summer Love

The snap of twigs and squirrels scatter,
Darting like red copper flame,
Seeking out their fruits of labour,
Leaving their burrows after the rain,
Sunshine and shadows on the lea,
Lovely is the earth in harmony.

Wind-chimes are tinkling out of sight,
So light a breeze, of sweetness through,
In nature's trail, and so entrancing,
Is the scent, of grass in the morning dew.
Land of fragrance, a lingering spell,
Happiness is - in the charm of a dell.

As slender saplings sway and whisper,
Firm, within their bed of green,
Dancing leaves are lit, by sunbeams,
And liquid skies in sapphire, stream.
Starlings, chirp in the trees above,
In a garden, rich in summer love.

Dorothy McGregor

Breathe For Me

In your own desolation
When you feel so utterly alone,
Close your eyes, tilt your face,
And feel the air around.

That which you breathe will fill your soul,
Sustain you through each day.

So see each gale as a driving force
To reach the next goal.
See each windless calm as reflection time
On who you really are.

You're never alone when you're alive,
You're part of this great world.

Leena Batchelor

The Dance Of Life

Life begins uncertainly
With a stumble and a fall
Slowly grows in confidence
From a fumbling crawl.
Learning, rushing into youth
Swirling with the throng
Dipping, swaying, bouncing,
Like a carefree song.
A discotheque of gaiety
Then a slower waltz
As burdens regulate the pace
And sweet dreams turn out false.
But inside, there still remains
The spirit of the dance
Tripping to life's metre
Of sadness and romance.
A measure of sedateness
Slows down the flighty fling
No longer mad gyrations
Which creeping age may bring.
Yet while a sparkle lingers
And there is still a chance
In spite of mind and body
The heart remains to dance.

Effie Dimmock

Do Try

Try to overlook those niggly things at home
That make the tempers fray, and raise the tone,
Look about, observe, the joys you have in store,
Don't lose them all along the way, or you will be a bore.

Try not to frown, and then maybe, to understand,
Not one of us is perfect, so do not be so grand.
A friendly word, instead of a shout, be kind
And honest as you talk; then try to unwind.

Try this, it will bring contentment, instead of strife,
You've probably got, if you know it, a lovely life,
Just think about these pleasant things, today,
Making happiness abound, that will last all the way.

Phyllis Wright

230

Summer

Evening shadows dance,
On water of silver
Carrying ripples of life away and away
Until they fade.

The knight in dazzling red armour
Strikes his many, golden swords
Down upon the lake so still.

Each sword reflects engraving
Of lives gone and life to come
And tells of all the happiness
Which has just begun
The words were very first
Engraved upon the hill,
Which time had carefully planned and written
And is writing still.
The words tell of ancient people who once lived on the land
And, of how this lake here today
Once did not stand
Like a mirror in the twilight
Which time holds in his hand.

Tracy L Webster

I See Myself

I see myself,
I am afraid
For all of the connections that I've made
Are not enough
For love
And all of that stuff.

Nicola Barnes

Togetherness

Yet each of us a barely glowing
Ember against the starry night,
Then together each and every one
And guide lost ships like harbour lights.

Though empty each and every lost soul feels
And a barren land the heart,
They too shall find their harbour lights
And they too shall have a part.

For alone, cold winds do cool our warmth
And cause our spirits wane.
Together gales can only serve
To feed our beckoning flame.

Lewis Lee

233

Around

Still here,
Just.
No lust,
 But
Still here,
So
 Why?
Nothing.
Still here
 Suspended -
In space
 No ace,
Still here.
Will do
 What?
Do not know
 But
Still here.

LPP

Chance

Chance is but a bubble rare,
A fragile crystal sphere
You hold awhile within your hands,
That soon will disappear.

Chance can open many doors
For one brief span of time.
The opportunity is yours
To take it or decline.

Chance can bring catastrophe,
Or make a life worthwhile.
Chance can break a person's hope,
Or make a loved one smile.

Chances large and chances small,
The action lies with you.
Would you try to grasp them all,
Or rather choose a few?

Should someone present to you
A globe of chance today,
Would you try its mystic power
Or throw the thing away?

Diana Duncan

Sunny Moments

The rays of the sun are warm and bright
Sometimes one sees birds in flight
Or, a child flying a kite
What a beautiful sight!

Jean Margaret Berry

Life

Life is for living
So go ahead,
Live -
Life to the full.
Give -
All you have to give.
No holding back
Lest you lose track
Of where you want to go
Or who you want to be.
Give life all you've got,
Forget about being
Content with your lot.
It's all up to you,
Try on the shoe
For size,
See how it fits.
Life's an experience,
Dance -
To the tune of life,
Spin -
Out of time with the world
And when you fall,
Exhausted,
You will know you have lived.

M S Reid

Faith

If in life you feel alone,
Hold on to faith to guide you home,
It will guide each day ahead,
Treading first the path you tread.

Faith will never let you down,
It will make the road firm ground,
Darkness turn to rays of light,
The world around shine very bright.

Have faith in each and every one,
Worry not - accept the way life comes,
Faith will lighten every hour,
Faith will be your staying power.

P Peet

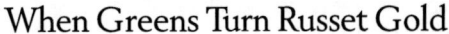

When Greens Turn Russet Gold

I have watched you crying
For your loved one far away
I know your heart is broken
Now hear the words I say.

The distance in between you
Cannot change that has been willed
To you, your love will return
When the summer's warmth has chilled.

Hush now, he will return to you
When greens turn russet gold
The summer warmth of your sweet love
Shall withstand the winter's cold.

Now dry away those teardrops
That trickle down your face
Soon he will show his depth of love
To you, in sweet embrace.

You are truly his beloved
Hold on to this, be strong
For when his travels finally cease
With you he will belong.

Marie Horridge

My Sanctuary

There is a place where I can go
When peace and calm I seek
A place where sand is soft and warm
Where lakes are clear and deep.

Water spills from craggy rocks
To tumble from great heights
And in the lush green undergrowth
The wandering streams delight.

Palm trees sweep around the bay
In paradise so sweet
Where breaking waves wash golden sand
And murmur in retreat.

In the clearing mists of dawn
I look upon the sea
And there a ship with windless sails
Drifts ghost-like; silently.

Far away an island lies
Shrouded in mystery
With towering cliffs and secret coves
It beckons; waits for me.

One day I'll go in open boat
To gaze on this new land
Where sun will shine from radiant heights
And warm the golden sand.

What I see is quickly gone
For this my sanctuary
Is but a fleeting glimpse beyond
It is my fantasy.

Martin Boyle

Untitled

Butterflies, butterflies all around
in the trees and on the ground
Flapping, flying everywhere
in the trees and in the air.

I love to watch them every day
having fun and all at play
I try to count them every day
they come so close then they fly away.

Butterflies, butterflies everywhere
flying around without a care
So please don't catch them
they are rare.

Helen Louisa Gray

Daily Grind

Please Lord make me understand
That *maybe* these are challenges
Set to encourage me
 to move forward
 however hard this may be
To persevere
 even on the darkest day
And to put my trust in Thee.

Mary A Slater

Friendship Song

Please be my friend
I need a friend, a very special friend.
One who is sad about my sorrow
And will be glad with me tomorrow.
A friend who'll be a friend throughout my life
Through hardship and in comfort, peace or strife.

Please be my friend
I need a friend, a very special friend.
Who bears with me my loneliness
Who shares in future happiness.
A friend who'll be my port in stormy seas
A friend who'll celebrate my smallest victories.

True friends would build on loyalty - and must
Be kindred spirits bonding through their trust
And understanding - in friendship lasting to the grave
They form the rock that can withstand the pounding of the wave.

Please be my friend
I need a friend, a very special friend.
Who'll sympathise when I despair
And will rejoice with me when all is fair.
A friend who'll be a friend in dire need
And be with me when Earth and Heaven meet.

Lisa Wolfe

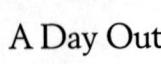

A Day Out

Children at the seaside,
Parents at their side,
'Mummy, Daddy'
'Can I have a ride?'
Walking round the fairground,
Eating candyfloss,
Riding on the dodgems,
Playing pitch and toss.
On the beach, castles in the sand
'Come on Daddy, give a helping hand.'
Paddling in the sea,
Riding on a donkey.
So much to see,
Also eating shellfish, 'Can I please
Have a bag of chips.'
'I'll take rock home for auntie,
She likes a stick.'
Watching the tide come in,
Saying 'Goodbye'
Leaving on the coach for home.
'What a lovely day!'

J Nicholls

Sunny Day

When sickness like a viper strikes
And venom starts to weave its way
Into the brave but weary soul;
What's called for is a sunny day.
So, sunny day stay with me,
If but a while you linger;
For you will gladden my sad heart
When dark clouds point their finger.
And when the storm has come to pass,
When I have lived through all the rain,
If I'm still weary, all I ask . . .
That you would shine for me again.

Marian Theodora Maddison

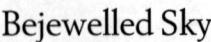

Bejewelled Sky

Millions of jewels in the sky
Like diamonds shine so bright
A contrast against the velvet sky
In the darkness of the night
Glittering, sparkling, twinkling stars
Shine down from a distant place
Just like a jewelled tapestry
Hung in time and space
It seems the ceiling of the sky
Designed by God's own hand
Is studded with these precious gems
As numerous grains of sand
This canopy of twinkling lights
Set in the velvet sky
The jewel box of the universe
Is scattered way up high.

Pat Bradley

When I Grow Up

When I grow up,
What will I be?
I could join the navy,
And sail out to sea.

When I grow up,
What will I do?
I could help lots of animals,
And work in a zoo.

When I grow up,
Will I go far?
I could become a pilot,
Or drive a racing car.

I won't go to sea,
Nor work in a zoo.
When I grow up,
I want to be like you.

Deanna L Dixon

Be Childlike

Be childlike, clown-like
Whatever it takes to help
Others around you
As you travel the road of life
For some a smile
Others a word of friendship.

Janet Glew

Faith - Love

God give me a heart
That's kind and true
Give me faith to walk with you
Give me courage to see things through
Hope and strength from you
To pursue, whatever
Path my feet must tread
May you be always at my head
When troubles knock at my door
You may open it, and love outpour
When I am weak, you are strong
That your love, for us all
Lasts our whole life long
You are there for our every need
So raise your eyes to the skies
God, will hear your prayer
And listen, take heed,
Comfort you, in times of need.
Have faith, believe, all will be well,
God is there, time will tell.

Amen.

Irene G Corbett

Never Feel Alone My Friend

Never feel alone my friend, there resting in your chair
The other chairs are empty, no one else is there.
So listen to the silence, that fills your cosy room
Let your imagination, hear the silence sing a tune.

Look upon the pictures, on the mantelpiece or wall
Let your imagination, hear again the voices call.
Have a little talk to them, no one else will know
Remember you're alone my friend, 'neath the candle glow.

Hear again the words they speak, from memories in your mind
Tell them all about your day, and pleasures you still find.
Cheer yourself throughout each day, you're never quite alone
Midst the old familiar things, and the pictures in your home.

Use those lovely memories in the album of your mind
With your imagination, they're always there to find.
Release again your memories, let imagination roam
In the peace and quiet, in the comfort of your home.

Donald Futer

God Speaks To *You!*

You are precious my child, and I love you,
So respect yourself and realise it's true,
Rejoice in the fact that you're special,
There's so much you, abiding in my love, can do.

You are chosen my child, and you're wanted,
Just rest in my arms and feel secure,
I need you to serve in my Kingdom,
To minister to both rich and poor

You are loved my child, and cherished,
So relax and enjoy my attention,
My mercy has cleansed every sin you've confessed,
They won't ever get a second mention.

You are unique my child, because I made you,
Perfectly formed, and perfectly known
By me, and as you trust in my care,
You will know my arms around you thrown.

Jane Otieno

Friendship

What is friendship?
I hear them say,
I hear this question,
Every day.

A friend is someone,
On whom you can rely.
A friend is someone,
Who will do or die.

A friend is someone,
Who makes you laugh.
They brighten you up
When you're feeling naff.

A friend is someone,
Who is willing to share.
A friend is someone,
Who really does care.

A friend is someone,
Who won't see you without.
A friend is someone,
Who is always about.

A friend is someone
Who is eager to please.
I feel very fortunate,
That you are all of these.

Roy Beaman

Picking Up The Pieces

My world has been torn to pieces,
my whole life came tumbling down.
How can I learn to live again,
now you're no longer around.

The building blocks of my life,
lay scattered on the ground.
The pain I feel is so unreal,
my worst nightmare came to town.

I can't get you out of my head,
I can't get you out of my mind.
No matter which way I turn,
the reality that once was you,
is nowhere to be found.

Help me Lord to pick up the pieces of my life,
and put them together one by one.
Somehow my life has to continue,
so for help I turn to God's own Son.

I pray, the Lord's outstretched hand is waiting,
to start the work that needs to be done.
For the sake of my own sanity, I put my faith
in God and Jesus alone.

Amen.

Robert Waggitt

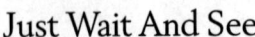

Just Wait And See

The rocky road of life
 is full of ups and downs,
it has its swollen rivers
 and many ways to drown,
like walking over thin cracked ice,
 with the water running deep,
just be careful where you're treading
 or you'll land up in a heap.

Life is not a bowl of cherries
 and never runs long smooth,
it is hard and nothing
 comes for naught,
so remember in your good times
 all the bad times you have had,
it's a lesson in your life
 that you've been taught.

So life is good on one day
 and lousy on the next,
that's the way it's been
 and everyone's the same,
so don't celebrate tomorrow
 till the present day is out,
you never know what's waiting . . .
 with your name.

Leslie Holgate

254

Tortoise

I am a tortoise.
I work at a plod-along pace,
Think hard about each laboured step I take
Though I'm clumsy,
Don't have too much grace.

Sometimes,
When others work faster,
I'm sad, feel that I'm a disgrace.
Till I stop and reflect and remember
It was the tortoise that won the race.

Joyce Walker

Today

Yesterday
My life was but a dream
For all my memories
From the past wanted to say hello
First to cruise my way
Was my first day at school
How I enjoyed the memory
Of me and my nephew
Skipping along with glee
Meeting all the other tots
Dressed in their fancy frocks
Little boys in their short pants
Their wobbly knees made me 'Huh'
Memories, fond memories
Made yesterday a day of gist
Today the mood is the same
Peaceful, sacred, divine
My daily reflections are jolly
I'm having fun all the time.

Caroline Pemberton

Telepathy

How can I reach you?
Will they give you
my Charms? -
Photographs
Poems
My letters and Cards?

How can I reach you
to tell you I care? -
Will the Waves of Telepathy
carry me there?

The Waves of Telepathy
are more strong than before,
the distant past gone
Destiny greets us once more -

But how can I reach you?
Let's wish on a Star -
then my arms will embrace you
'Wherever' you are.

Mary Skelton

A Life In A Day

Watching clouds drift slowly across the sky
I think like a day how quickly life passes by
It doesn't seem that long, but when you look back
You realise how far you've travelled down life's track
Child, to youth, with spirit reckless and free
The problems of being grown up, are yet to be
Summers were long, Christmas always had snow
Positive pictures in your mind of times long ago
These were times to enjoy, you had not a care
Biggest problems concerned your clothes and your hair
Yes when growing up there is not much strife
This is the morning of your life.

Then you meet someone special and if luck's on your side
She feels the same way and becomes your bride
Children will follow, bring with them unbridled joy
Irrelevant whether it be a girl or a boy
Your childhood behind you, now you're a man
It doesn't really matter at what age it began
You now have the love of a wife and offspring
But the cost to pay is the responsibility it will bring
Knowing young defenceless innocent lives depend mainly on you
Makes this the most stressful time that you will go through
But your babies soon grow, they will be adults soon
It seems just in a wink of an eye, gone is your life's afternoon.

Early evening now, your fledglings have flown the nest
Together you've probably got through life's sternest test
First lovers, then parents, you now become closer as friends.
More time to enjoy each other before the darkness descends
Then a new generation of special people start to appear
Grandchildren for you both to love and hold dear
Bringing their own unique pleasure to you and your wife.
A fresh dawn to you both in the twilight of life

It's getting late, not much time left, night is beginning to fall
Don't waste it on quarrels that mean nothing at all
And when midnight strikes, your life's over, I hope like myself
you can say
Please don't grieve for me my friends, I've had a wonderful day.

258   *Alan Edwards*

Smile Your Worries Away

I look in the mirror
Each and every day
But never really see
Just what has come my way

I look in the mirror
And wonder why
Lonely tears
I do cry

There is no need
There is no need
Look again
Take heed! Take heed!

You are not alone
Look again! Look again!
There is no need
For all that pain

We all have
A shining star
It guides us from
So very far

So when in the
Mirror you reflect
Don't be filled
With regret

Smile - just smile
And to yourself say
This is going to
Be *my day!*

Tricia Layton

Untitled

Life can be happy
life can be sad
Life can be weary
but never that bad

Count all your blessings
the next time you're kissed
On each shooting star
remember to wish

Always be thankful
for people you know
Give someone a smile
wherever you go

You can make a difference
by shining a light
A positive motion
will help you feel right

Experience beauty
from inside and out
This is really
what life's all about.

Deborah Hall

What's For You, Won't Go By You

Every day we live in hope,
That from somewhere will come a rope.
To pull us from our deepening rut,
Or open doors that once were shut.
Instead of living life to full,
We want some way to change the rule

Checking numbers weekly in anticipation you will find,
A winning combination to leave the past behind.
Waiting for that surprise call or letter,
That's going to make things so much better.
Don't wish upon that distant star,
Look at things the way they are.

By accepting what may come along,
Which could be right, not always wrong
Learn to live with what you've got,
Not what you might be given.
Then what looked like hell the week before,
May next week seem like heaven.

Jim Fraser

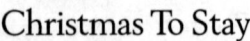

Christmas To Stay

The leaves are browning ready to fall
Summer's leaving and I don't worry at all
It means winter's near and what comes then?
The time of good cheer
It's Christmas again.
When the reindeer fly
All so high in the sky
Bringing Santa upon his sleigh
Loading stockings and filling under trees
Getting ready for the perfect day.
Tinselled rooms, outside's lighted bright
Feeling the Christmas spirit in full flight
Smiling children scamper from their bed
Gift wrap paper being torn in shreds
The sound of laughter drowns the singing of birds
And only nice things said can be heard
Crackers a-banging and bellies at full stretch
The smiling child teaching puppy to fetch
Christmas pud, roasted chestnuts
Lots of helping hands, no ifs or buts
Families together, perhaps once a year
Talking about old times over a beer
No worry of work and all its stress
Just loads of fun and lots of mess
Oh could you just love Christmas every day
Perhaps the next one could be made to stay?

Pete Simmons

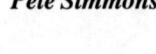

262

Life Is Too Short

Life is too short for any vain regretting!
Let the dead bury its dead, I say,
And let us go upon our way forgetting
The joys and sorrow of each yesterday
Between the sun's rising and its setting
We have not time for useless tears of fretting.
Life is too short.

Life is for any bittering feelings!
Time is the best avenger if we wait.
The years speed by, and on winging bear
We have no room for anything like hate,
This solemn truth the low mounds seem relating
That think and fast about our feet are steaking,
Life is too short.

Life is too short for aught but endeavour
Too short for spite but long enough for love
And links the worlds that circle on above
'Tis God first law, the universe's sign never.
Life is too short!

M S Cornbill

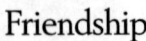

Friendship

I have a good friend in you
You cheer me up, when I'm down or feeling blue.
We've know each other for many years
Through lots of laughter,
Some sadness and tears.
But we are always here for each other.
And a better friend, I could not find another.
You always seem to understand,
And always lend a helping hand.
Our friendship forever will be
Because I have a good friend in you,
And you have a good friend in me.

Trudie Sullivan

264

A Secret Place

I know a place
Where only I go
To think and plan
What I shall do
Tomorrow - a secret place

I know a place
Where we go
You and I
I take you there
To my - secret place

I know a place
Which is happy and warm
For family and friends
At my - secret place

I know a place
I first visited long ago
Now I go often
To my - secret place

I know a place
Which can change each day
Sometimes near
Sometimes away
My - secret place

I know a place
I could tell you about
Hush! I close my eyes
And I am in
'A Secret Place'.

Pauline Bamber

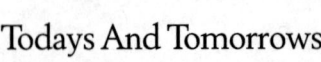

Todays And Tomorrows

You may think about tomorrow as you sit down today
Tomorrow may bring some magic, a surprise, your holiday
You look forward to the future but you really have no idea
You can plan how it might be without favour without fear
Will it bring long-term happiness or will it bring a war?
Will it be what you and she were always hoping for?
Well, tomorrow came and she was gone, dead at forty-nine
And into the bottomless pit I fell for a very very long time.

But one day I managed to climb out, I met you a bright new star
As for a long time in those tomorrows, I could not see that far
And you gave me back my todays and helped me dream new dreams
Those tomorrow dreams we now share as life goes on, it seems.
And now we're three with a small new boy who was born on
                                                just a today

He did not come tomorrow, neither yesterday
Now he's two and we are planning for a holiday
Tomorrow, but when we fly out it will be a today

Tomorrow never comes they say to use a hackneyed phrase
The truth is that tomorrow is just an unknown future today
Go ahead! Do it now even if it doesn't come entirely right
Unless you do it right now you may never see the light
Even with my child I know I must try today and shine
His tomorrows are many. Who knows the length of time?
I have learned the hard way that you can dream and plan away
But if there's no tomorrow at least you did it all today.

Mike Jackson

266

The Rainbow Of Life

Red is the vibrant colour of life
As we go through our childhood years
Symbolising the voyage of great discovery
When we have no worries or fears

Orange is the dawning of maturity
When our minds turn to other things
We realise those stories of birds and bees
Didn't just mean that they have wings

Yellow represents the gradual calming
As our impetuous youth is left behind
The responsibilities of adult life
Are suddenly impressed on our minds

Green is the natural abundance of life
When our young crop is growing up fast
We see in them what we used to have
And we pray that their happiness will last

Blue is the period of thinking back
When we spend all our time reminiscing
We enviously watch the emerging youth
And rue the good times which we're missing

Indigo is the dusk of our lifelong day
We relax from all anguish and strife
We give each other the love which we'll need
For the impending sunset of life

Violet is the end of our lifelong year
We finally meet the cold of December
But we leave behind us a rainbow of colours
Which we hope that our young will remember.

Enrico

267

An Evening At Home

The work that fills my every day,
I leave behind with kindly pleasure.
The sky outside that's dull and grey,
Brings thoughts of home and cosy leisure.

I see our bright lit window there,
My family with their cheery greeting.
Mum's evening meal of homely fare,
With talk and laughter whilst we're eating.

Our well-loved dog lies by the fire,
The warmth that curves around us there
Leaves nothing more I could desire,
Than this dear home that we all share.

The doorbell rings, friends come inside
We talk of many things,
Make plans for coming Christmastide,
And all the fun that it will bring.

Then when I lie warm in my bed,
I thank my God for all his care.
Outside bright stars are overhead,
More pleasure that we all can share.

Betty Smyth

Lost On Earth. Found In Heaven. September 11th 2001

Tonight my love the tears like rain are falling,
and rent the hearts and minds and souls apart,
within that darkest void left with thy passing,
upon God's ocean a new life I must chart
and through the hell and anguish and the torment,
I'll damn them all, what more can I say,
for night is guaranteed to bring tomorrow,
yet life it seems ended here today.
And yet I know you're there beyond the mortal,
to walk with me where silent footsteps fall,
and shadows cast on pavements by the moonlight,
awakes my soul to answer to thy call.
And memories shall help me face each morning,
upon the wind, I'll hear you call my name,
and bridges bridged by bridges they will take me,
and loose the shackles that mortal life does claim.
Yet boldly will I tread the paths I wander,
guided by thy spirit on my way,
God must have wanted roses in his garden,
so many precious blooms he picked today.
Tread softly then, await my final calling,
and as for me I know life must go on,
so many stars tonight were born in Heaven,
we watch them shining brightly, each and every one.

J Brohee

269

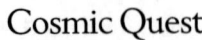

Cosmic Quest

Every day
I vainly try
to find some significance
in the daily
trivia
which confines us
each waking second
each minute each hour
each day each week
each month each year
that we exist
upon this sad polluted World.

I try to comprehend
this tiny grain of matter
called planet Earth
our parent star the Sun
our Milky Way gathering of stars
trillions of other galaxies
the Cosmos the Universe
Time Space Matter
and the dimension
of ultimate Infinity
and I strive to discover
our human future in the scheme.

I believe that in
the immensity of space
the answer lies
and when we reach that point
we will become a sentient part
of the living cosmological whole.

Stephen Gyles

Raise The Sails

On this day
when time and tide are right.
Step down upon the pebble beach,
walk slowly to the shore.
Take up the mooring and pull the boat in.
On this day,
when grey skies fill with ill-intent,
step aboard.
Untie the ropes, the bonds that root you to this place,
and cast them to the waves.
Raise the sails and let them swell with unbridled might.
And on this day,
set no course, but merely,
like a feather on a pond, let nature do her bidding.
Accept her fate, and pander to her naked whim.
And on this day,
if those scudding skies of love and hate
take you back to shore, then sail no more,
for you will have truly found your home.

Andy Colley

271

Autumnal

The moon rises now,
Gilding cloud edges,
Dropping wisp like curls,
Upon the roofs,
Silently.

Where the shadows lie,
A bright pool of light,
Reflects, the moonbeams,
Glimmering there,
Quietly.

Below the night life,
Uncoiling serpent,
Slithers cunningly,
Stealthily.

The darkness descends,
A velvet curtained,
Angel of mercy,
Soothingly.

Then the sun rises,
A phoenix of flame,
Waking up the earth,
Hopefully.

Kathleen M Scatchard

Wisdom Of Prayer

The wisdom of prayer comes from within.
There is a need for prayers in certain situations
And circumstances.

It may be because of the sad loss of loved ones
Or a need to do well at something,
Or a need for a cure to an incurable disease,
Such as cancer.
It could also be a thank you prayer
Or a prayer for forgiveness.

There are many reasons for prayers,
Mainly a need to exercise strong feelings
And to have God near.

It can be taught.
It can be short.
But do it with feeling and sensible thought.
For the wisdom of prayer cannot be bought
But within you is where it is caught.

Don't worry if it all comes to nought
You should feel partially better,
That is what you ought.
And if everything comes together of sorts
Think of God and what he is about.
That is important without a doubt.

Ali Sebastian

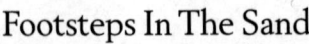

Footsteps In The Sand

One night a man had a dream.
He dreamed he was walking along the beach with the *Lord.*
Across the sky flashed scenes from his life.
For each scene, he noticed two sets of footprints in the sand:
one belonging to him, and the other to the *Lord.*

When the last scene of his life flashed before him
he looked back, at the footprints in the sand.
He noticed that many times along the path of his life
there was only one set of footprints.
He also noticed that it happened at the very lowest and
saddest times
of his life.

This really bothered him and he questioned the *Lord* about it:
'Lord, you said that once I decided to follow you,
you'd walk with me all the way.
But I have noticed that during the most troublesome times in my life
there is only one set of footprints.
I don't understand why when I needed you most you would leave me.'

The *Lord* replied:
'My son, My precious child, I love you and I would never leave you,
During your times of trial and suffering,
when you see only one set of footprints, it was then that I carried you.'

Anon

The Gift Of Friendship

Friendship is the only gift we wish to have returned.
Returned only by those who value its true meaning -
Invisible, yet illustrious. Forceful whilst frail.
Easily destroyed, though solid and enduring.
Never take it in selfishness, or with triviality.
Deliver it humbly, using caution and forethought.
Strong is the framework when built with sincerity:
Holding the contents, delicate and complex.
Ignore all the flaws, imperfections and defects.
Pass on the gift and celebrate if returned!

Sandra Wolfe

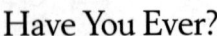

Have You Ever?

Have you ever wondered why it is
That certain folk are slow to credit
Some others on their achievements?
And why it is that these self-same folk
Will spare no opportunity and
Waste not a moment to praise
To the rafters *others* whose contributions
Are modest in the extreme or by comparison?
Have you felt even a trifle despised or humiliated
When having worked your seat off
There is not the slightest mention
Of your work or effort, and yet with
The other guy, there's radiance from the rear end?
How is it then that these folk make their choices
About who deserves their attention and accolade
While other deserving beings need barely be acknowledged?
Have you not had the experience of being denied
Any credit when, in fact, your thoughts and ideas
And suggestions were crucial in producing desired results?
Have you never witnessed the phenomenon of 'I'
When the person responsible for a positive outcome
Seeks to obtain all the adulation
Yet it's 'we' when you, in actual fact, did it all?
Have you never - even sometimes - come across this
And felt ever so sore about it? Have you ever?

Francis de Lima

276

The Loved One

When morning comes
I shall return to the day
Ready for another
remembrance on your
inward gaze of memory
Forever held dear in your
precious eyes

Call to me and I will come
on the wind.
And speak to your heart
A message of farewell
For only your ears and lips to
behold.
Knowing I am a pause
Away from you.
Listening to your heartbeat
carried to me by
the wind's kind breeze.
That carries you to me
across the Great Divide
of life and rest.

Go well amid the hubbub of life.
Be gentle to yourself,
and know I am listening
to your heartbeat
entwined with mine forever.

I cherish you
in the arms that no longer
breathe the mortal
breath of life.
Go well dear heart
And know that I love you
forever as you draw
breath and beyond rejoined
anew.

Zing Rock

So Impulsive - Crystal Light

The violent storm, crescendos high
To hear the crack of thundering sky!
As I behold, such a beautiful sight,
A crystal vase, radiates, such lights,
So many varied, shimmering colours,
As streaking sun, flows thro' glass and delights
Crimsons, sapphire blues, green emeralds shine
Reflections flicker, make heads incline,
Perceptions, eyes, encompass all
Terrific pages, of light unfurl
Rainbows shower on every pearl
Of light sent streaming, minds a'whirl.
Suddenly, a cloud appears
Then all is lost from sight, just disappears
All that beauty of such sunshine glow
So lets my room gain sheer delight
Decorated by Master's hand, so right
Here now, I await, my sunshine guest
To lend my life, full of work - amazed
Bringing shields of champions - raised
Another vision, my home invades
To show me once again
My Lord's presence, still remains.

A Boddison

Mug

I could measure my life in coffee spoons
each one a stir from the past
Sweet, not bitter
Smooth but never rich
Often dark
an aromatic blend of memories
(a little froth would be nice)
I have measured my life in coffee spoons
and none of them were for me
I only drink tea!

Sarah Hardy

Coming To Terms

What does it take to get through the day
When the ones you have lived for are gone?
Finding the strength to go forward again
As Life goes relentlessly on.
A lifetime of beautiful memories
Is never enough you see
Because I loved them all so much
The same as they loved me.
But I am blessed with their goodness
Such happiness I can recall.
Their loving touch and warm embrace
Is what I miss most of all.
I'm sure someone watches over me
In a strangely wonderful way.
Leading me on to pastures new,
Giving a lift to my day.
Time has taught me many things
At last I can understand
That through the long and lonely years
I am held in the palm of God's hand.

Enid Rathbone

Why Wait Until Tomorrow?

Why wait until tomorrow
When a lot can be achieved today
Why path the same mistakes
When you can take another way

The future is not ours to decide
We must do what we can with God on our side
Make amends with those against us
Strive to improve our lives for the better, work hard
to gain more
And find that special someone you've been looking for

Travel and acquaint yourself with every person you meet
Attain knowledge and understanding
And maybe try a crazy feat
Be positive and aim for your best
And in due circumstances attempt to impress

Do something that makes you feel good
And will influence others too
Make something right, finish the undone
Achieve a task you've long dreamed of, make merry
and have fun
Life's too short to worry about the past
Tomorrow is a long way away so make the present last.

Mary Ibeh

New Hope

You must find it in the towering trees
Find it in the morning breeze
Find it in the garden weeds
And in the sowing of new seeds
New Hope
Your heart so heavy so made of pain
Must be made to lighten again
And the thoughts that never stop at all
Must stop, for you've given this your all
Or you're destined for ruin
And deserve all you get
For you live or you die, but to forget
Your lover was false, your faith is gone
Your future is empty, no laughter no song
You feel but self-pity, absorbs all your mind
For the millions who suffer, you say 'Be kind'
You eyes are opened on the suffering of the world
Was it yesterday you were softly curled
In the arms of a loved one you trusted and knew
To be faithful and honest, humble and true
Deceit is a word and revenge instant armour
But the hurt only hurts the more
For the strength to go on you would give all your wealth
But the fear in your heart is destroying your health
You must fight this battle and win and win
For to lose this one would be a sin
For the ones who need you would be hurt
So let's start off fighting for them with a spurt
It doesn't matter if you don't succeed
Or if you can't supply their need
What matters is you try with all that you've got
And your life isn't wasted, it's not, it's not.

Phyllis Shotton

A Lesson From The Sunflowers

Autumn has arrived and it is time to visit the local schools to take morning assemblies. I am quite excited at this prospect because I want to tell the children about our wonderful sunflowers!
We raised and grew three strong sunflowers from seed.
They were carefully transplanted into a prepared bed.
Each was given the same tender loving care but each one developed uniquely different.
Our three flowers varied in height from one and a half metres to three metres high, despite coming out of the same packet of seeds.
The head of the tallest weighed several pounds and was bigger than a large dinner plate.
The individuality of the flowers reminded me of the uniqueness of each child. The children share the same teachers.
They have the same academic environment but each develops at a different pace and achieves different standards.
I wonder if I can impress upon the children how unique and special they are? God loves them whatever their size or ability and each is precious in His sight.

Thelma Robinson

Reflections

Reflect only the most positive views:
People we meet, those whom we choose.
Reflect love and peace a world to inspire,
Compassion and hope for those who require.
Come the day such light to see
Reflections of others, reflections of me.

Audrey Ducharme

Don't

Don't cross the rainbow
If it's shaded grey
It takes you to a lonely place
Where colour has faded away.

Don't watch the skyline
If it's painted red
A storm of anger
When pollution spreads.

Don't touch the flowers
Guarded by a thorn
Recreates a crying sorrow
When your heart is torn.

Don't cross the rainbow
If it's clearer than glass
Live each day for the future
Stop living in the past.

Simon P Hewitt

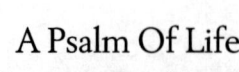

A Psalm Of Life

Tell me not in mournful numbers,
Life is but an empty dream!
For the soul is dead that slumbers,
And things are not what they seem.

Life is real! Life is earnest!
And the grave is not its goal;
Dust thou are, to dust thou returnest,
Was not spoken of the soul.

Not enjoyment, and not sorrow,
Is our destined end or way;
But to act, that each tomorrow
Find us farther than today.

Art is long, and Time is fleeting,
And our hearts, though stout and brave,
Still, like muffled drums, are beating
Funeral marches to the grave.

In the world's broad field of battle,
In the bivouac of Life,
Be not like dumb, driven cattle!
Be a hero in the strife!

Trust no Future, howe'er pleasant!
Let the dead Past bury its dead!
Act - act in the living Present!
Heart within, and God o'erhead!

Lives of great men all remind us
We can make our lives sublime,
And, departing, leave behind us
Footprints on the sand of time;

Footprints, that perhaps another,
Sailing o'er life's solemn main,
A forlorn and shipwrecked brother,
Seeing, shall take heart again.

Let us then be up and doing,
With a heart for any fate;
Still achieving, still pursuing,
Learn to labour and to wait.

Henry Wadsworth Longfellow

286

Haberdashery

I came upon 'Petticoat Lane',
London's market of renowned fame.
A busier, colourful, lively scene;
My eyes had never seen.

Second-hand books, second-hand clothes,
Trinkets, knick-knack on stall exposes.
Porcelain, brass and hardware,
Spoiled for choice, bargains everywhere.

I came upon a different stall,
The most striking of them all.
'Haberdashery' the bright sign said.
Intrigued, I looked at the display.

Ribbons, hats' pins and reels of cottons,
Epaulettes, frilly laces, an array of buttons.
The pearly buttons were lovely things
Fitted for Pearly Queens and Kings.

'Haberdashery' an unheard word for me
As I am a native across the sea.
Pearly Queens and Kings, I never saw before
Until I spotted them in a Haberdashery Store!

Licia Johnston

Friendship

Seek not perfection in another
Hope not for love that wavers never
Don't wait for hands to offer help
Or you may wait for ever.

Expect no gifts from those you give
Do not be hurt by thoughtless words
Forbear with those who would live, as you
Heed not what you should not have heard.

Take this advice I offer, and
Follow it, I promise in the end
You will possess that quality
That makes all men desire you for a Friend.

A Wheeler

To Autumn

Season of mists and mellow fruitfulness,
      Close bosom-friend of the maturing sun;
Conspiring with him how to load and bless
      With fruit the vines that round the thatch-eves run;
To bend with apples the moss'd cottage trees,
      And fill all fruit with ripeness to the core;
    To swell the gourd, and plump the hazel shells
  With a sweet kernel; to set budding more,
And still more, later flowers for the bees,
Until they think warm days will never cease,
      For summer has o'er-brimm'd their clammy cells.

Who hath not seen thee oft amid thy store?
      Sometimes whoever seeks abroad may find
Thee sitting careless on a granary floor,
      Thy hair soft-lifted by the winnowing wind;
Or on a half-reap'd furrow sound asleep,
      Drows'd with the fume of poppies, while thy hook
  Spares the next swath and all its twined flowers:
And sometimes like a gleaner thou dost keep
      Steady thy laden head across a brook;
      Or by a cyder-press, with patient look,
  Thou watchest the last oozings hours by hours.

Where are the songs of spring? Ay, where are they?
      Think not of them, thou hast thy music too -
While barren clouds bloom the soft-dying day,
      And touch the stubble plains with rosy hue;

Then in a wailful choir the small gnats mourn
      Among the river sallows, borne aloft
      Or sinking as the light wind lives or dies;
And full-grown lambs loud bleat from hilly bourn;
    Hedge-crickets sing; and now with treble soft
    The red-breast whistles from a garden croft;
    And gathering swallows twitter in the skies.

John Keats

289

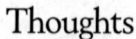

Thoughts

A garden filled with beauty fair
Brings one great peace beyond compare
A garden filled with flowers seems
The epitome of all my dreams
Sweet peas foxgloves - roses too
Reds and yellows - shades of blue
Beauty unmatched in all its glory
Just one part of nature's story
But winter brings its savage climes
Round about the cold wind winds
Again to spring one's thoughts will fly
The beauty gone - again is nigh
And so full circle turns the wheel
Of nature's sentence and repeal
So savage - yet its tender kiss
Fills one's heart with perfect bliss.

T C Hollis

Serenity

Sitting high up in my tree, the wind does gently blow,
I look around at all the things my eyes see far below,
Greenest grass and sky so blue, people all around,
I sit so high up in my tree I cannot hear a sound.
Except for sweetest birdsong, it tinkles in my ears,
Calms my mind, removes all thought, takes away my fears
And as I sit with heart of joy, hearing birds' refrain,
I am so glad to be right here, gone is all my pain.
Then suddenly the wind does rise and tree begins to sway,
The ocean rises higher now not so far away,
Swirling darkened water covers over grass of green
Till all is angry tempest, no grass left to be seen.
People are all fighting looking upwards to my tree,
Howling madly, eyes all glazed, wishing to be free.
My eyes are wide with disbelief at all the hate I feel
Pouring from the people, my eyes begin to reel.
Still my tree supports me, holds me gently in its arms,
Leaves do whisper to me they are keeping me from harm.
Water leaping high now trying to dislodge my seat
Slaps and moans and twists around, soaking through my feet,
Pain from realising all the things I failed to see
Even though within myself 'twas simply not to be.
As mind joins deep with heart now, I put the pain away,
Knowing deep within my core it cannot in here stay.
Then, as the knowing deepens, wind begins to die a death,
So once again all I can hear are whispers of my breath,
Birds again are singing their true and wondrous sound
And from my lofty perch I see less people on the ground,
Serenity returns now, no more down there I play
Within my gentle branches, it's here I plan to stay.

Marsha Durok

Lake-Land

Sweet breeze, of fragrance,
A rousing song on fell and glade,
By nature's trail, a stream of sunbeams,
The bonny bluebells, dance, in shade.

A sight to gladden every heart,
A mist, upon the mountains,
Shifting skies of haunting hues,
And pools of dark green satin.

Bathed, in yellow gold and silver,
An arch, of the sun's bright rays,
Sequins sparkling on deep waters,
A lovely vision, the lakes, embrace.

Dorothy McGregor

If

If my words could cross the empty space
That lies between you and I
I would let you know I love you so
And how so much I cry
If my arms could reach beyond
This realm we call reality
I would wrap them tight around you
To keep you here with me
If my eyes could see in the darkness
And my feet walk back through time
I would walk night and day, come what may
Until the day when you were mine.

Eileen Feerick

New Song

You've put a new song in my mouth
A song I did not know
My mind was dark, my heart was cold,
My life was full of woe.
His worthy Name I could not sing
No offering of praise could bring.

I tried to worship as I ought
To praise a God divine.
But when I tried my lips were dumb
This Lord, He was not mine.
His worthy Name I could not sing
No offering of praise could bring.

And then I saw Him lifted high
A crown of thorns He wore.
He suffered on that cruel tree
When all my sins He bore.
His worthy Name I start to sing
An offering of praise to bring.

My darkened mind He filled with light
My heart He opened wide.
'Come unto me that you might live'
This loving Saviour cried.
His worthy Name at last to sing
An offering of praise to bring.

A sinner saved by sovereign grace
To Him I raise my voice.
Because of all He's done for me
I cannot but rejoice.
His worthy Name I'll ever sing
An offering of praise to bring.

Patricia Patterson

Recollections

The autumn leaves are falling as
I walk down the lane.
The rustic leaves are crushed by the
tread of feet again.

Memories some flooding back of days
so long ago.
When I would skip along this same old
lane in sunshine and in snow.

Just think in years to come, children
not yet born;
Will skip along this same old lane,
I hope with the same old fun.

Arnold A Monk

Snaps

Listen.
Universes constructed
From a handful of words -
Lanzarote,
Tenerife,
Twycross Zoo,
Paraglide,
Bungee jump,
Surf the Seven Seas,
Did you have a good time?

From your holiday
Reminiscings
I will build
My castles in the air -
Enchanted words
To give my mind release
Visiting places
Where my feet
Can leave no mark.

Keep talking.
Let my mind
Roam free -
As free as your words -
Soaring, plunging,
Poised,
Swooping suddenly,
Vicariously visiting
The furthest crevice
Of the globe.

Lynn M Cochrane

296

The Music Of My Heart

When life just seems so pointless,
Full of sadness and of gloom,
And the only music that I hear
Proclaims my nearby doom,
I turn my ears away from the world
And find a brand new start,
With melodies and harmonies
That live within my heart.
I hear a tune of happiness
That soon becomes my song
Which leads me through my troubled times
And says it won't be long
Until the sun will shine again
And I will smile once more,
No longer mourn for those who chose
To push me out the door.
Though my heart sinks low, my voice sings high
The way it always should,
Reminding me that one day soon
My life will turn to good.
My heartstrings strum a tune of peace
While the voices in my head
Sing joyously and carry me
When my heart is as heavy as lead.
So whenever I'm feeling really low
And the tears begin to start,
I turn from life and listen to
The music of my heart.

Jacqueline Howard

Autumn Leaves

'The leaves are changing colour - now
the year is growing old,

From many different shades of
green - to rusty-red and gold,

Some have started falling, with a
gentle rustling sound,

And in profusion lay there - a
carpet on the ground.'

Dot Stubbs

The Gift Of Time

Dear Lord,
Today I will give myself
The gift of time
With You,
I will put aside
All worries and cares
And sit quietly
With You.
I will empty my mind
Of all worldly thoughts
And think only
Of You,
I will then lovingly wrap
This precious gift
Of time with You,
And carry it with me
Throughout the day.

Helena Abrahams

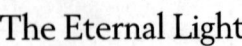

The Eternal Light

I'm afraid I've lost the connection
The light that I know
The perfection that I am
The Godhead which is within.
Instead of radiating light
I surround myself with grey
But the embers remain
Waiting to be ignited.
A familiar warmth stirs
It was all an illusion
As the flame never went out.

Janet Rocher

The Bud Of Love

The bud of love lies
Within each person's heart;
In some hearts is it so
Tightly closed, the warmth
Enfolded far too deeply
Within to open out the
Petals. In others, the bud
Is beginning to open in
Various stages of unfoldment;
In the rare heart it has
Long ceased to be a bud,
But lives fully open
Sending out its fragrance
Into the whole universe,
Its perfume lingering
On everything it contacts.

Elizabeth Anandadeva

One World, One People

One world, one people, one power, one love
The power of the Lord all over the world
Have we really tried enough
One life is all we're given
To make of as we will
One heart full of hope unending
One wish we must fulfil
One dream that seems eternal
Since this old world began
Dignity and understanding
And compassion for each man
So far it all seems sorrow and bloodshed
All the way, where is that shiny bright tomorrow
We are praying for today?
One world, one people, one power, one love,
The power of the Lord all over the word
Have we really tried enough?
                Have we really tried enough?

A Reed

The Blind Man

Today I passed a blind man
Who had halted by the kerb
He stood, apparently listening
To the traffic, trying to raise the nerve
To cross the road at a safe time
Then he stepped out, with stick held high
While I, to my eternal shame
With averted eyes, just passed him by

Since then it's preyed upon my mind
That I showed such lack of care
For I have always lived a Christian life
Trying to be both just and fair
Could it be I feared rejection
If I should have offered him my aid?
No, that would be a poor excuse
The truth was my plans were made

For my days were once ruled by the clock
As I dashed both here and there
Always trying to meet new deadlines
It seemed I had no time to spare
Now that blind man's brought me to a halt
And my life to re-evaluate
Now I will take the time to live once more
At a pace that is more sedate.

Don Woods

Hand On Heart

Can you put your hand on heart.
And say that you've been good?
Can you speak with truthful words,
You've done the best you could?

Trekking on life's varied paths,
Have you helped a friend?
Did you give him comfort,
And your ear, did lend?

When the old were lonely,
Did your time vacate?
Though your mind was elsewhere,
Did you stop and conversate?

Have you entertained the young,
With patience and goodwill?
Sat with someone reading,
When that soul was ill?

Has your life been generous,
To those with lesser fates?
Do you give a helping hand,
Never needing self rebates?

Can you put your hand on heart,
When it's time to go?
Will your memory, be cherished,
Only people left will know.

Duchess Newman

304

Autumn

Every season has its beauty,
Has its colours, has its moods,
Wrought by God they ring the changes,
Making everything brand new.

Days for planting, weeks for growing,
Spring and summer brightly dressed,
Sparkling whiteness in the winter,
But it's autumn I love best.

Autumn garners all the goodness
Of the months that go before,
Then it adds a hint of sadness
For the past will come no more.

Gone the brightness, gone the glory,
Autumn's tones are brown and gold,
Yet the trees with fruit are laden
To sustain us through the cold.

So in nature, as in living,
All our middle years abound
With God's blessings tinged by sadness,
Just like autumn all year round.

Sheila Burnett

The Shepherd

In the hush of the westering, evening sun,
The sheep graze, peaceful and still.
The shepherd, his weathered face aglow,
Watches his flock on the hill.

He sees the little black lamb disappear,
Where a gap in the hedge has been made.
He hears its mother's frightened cry,
Beseeching him, begging his aid.

In quick, long strides he clears the gate,
Scoops up the lamb in his arm,
Returns it to its mother's side
And all again is calm.

'I am the Shepherd,' Lord, You said,
And Mary pleads for me.
Lift me, Your black sheep, through the gate
That leads to Heaven and Thee.

Mary Robertson

Still Centre

There is a skill
In standing still,
Being your own calm centre.
Dropping the world off,
Shrugging away the rush,
Sidelining the pavement's
Shove and push.
The blur of buses,
The pedestrian's panic
And car's cacophony,
Where the shopping's manic,
Can cease,
If you sincerely long for peace.
Be like a standing stone,
A quiet, wise rock,
Be steady and reposed,
Able to withstand all shock.
Let the spinning around you
Swirl out of control,
Be firm and singular
Keep your sanity whole.
Whisper away the world
In your own silence,
Unravel the harmony
From a mad day's nonsense.

Keith Melbourne

Autumn Clouds

Great grey clouds sail
the autumn sky,
low above earth they
sail slowly by;

Over town and field
but no one looks up
to see these giants
go sailing by;

Beggar man, poor man
rich man, thief -
all miss this armada
of clouds in the sky.

Michael Rowson

Rise Up

I look on all I see and do,
I live my life to be with you
And over all my ways, take hold of me,
This I ask of you.

I look on what is in my life,
I see a world so full of strife,
And in the moments left within my time,
This I ask of you.

And I will rise up, rise up,
There on angels' wings,
And I will rise up, rise up,
And raise myself to you.

I look to see a better place,
So that we all may sit in grace,
And as I try to walk the path of truth
This I ask of you.

And I will rise up, rise up,
There on angels' wings,
And I will rise up, rise up,
And raise myself to you.

John Cook

Storm

I ride on the eye of the storm and embrace the cold force of
the whirling wind.
I laugh as it blows my hair and forces tears from my eyes.
I am powerless as my breath is sucked away into the night and
My thirst is sated by the power of the rain as it refuses to desist.
Later, when the storm abates, the sun lights my path and warms
 my skin.
The sand on my feet is washed away by the tides of the great ocean.
A gentle breeze replaces the anger of the morning wind,
Causing the multicoloured flowers to bow their heads in welcome
as I pass.
Soon, far away in another kind of time, the moon will smile
affectionately and light my way.
Another day, another storm, another season.

Liz Barkes

A Time To Reflect

I sit in this tranquil place
And cast my eyes across
Nature's bounteous life.
Rolling hills and valleys,
Trees that embrace
The warm glistening sun,
Celebrating the autumnal
Spectrum of colour.
God's artistry swept over a world
That is gifted with a vision
Of peace and love,
Where worship unites us in spirit
And forgiveness is our blessing.

Sue Umanski

In Your Trouble

Oh my friend - I know not why - but I wish it need not be so
Yet, somehow from this wasteland I feel that life will flow.
A different sort of life perhaps, new and deeper than before
The God of mercy will provide an ever-opening door.
His hand in yours to guide and bless, to succour and give peace
Your trusting soul, though in turmoil now, will find blessings
that never cease
It's you who have given help to people before, with kindness over
 many years
You've always tried hard and given your best - how I wish I could
calm your fears.
For fears there are, I know you agree - for that is the nature of things
It's a matter of taking one step at a time, just seeing what each
day brings
But always remember a new way may be found - tomorrow - you
just never know
So, look upward and outward and say to yourself, 'I'll only let joyful
thoughts grow'
You've always been brave and though now you need help, I'm sure
that your courage will stay
You'll continue to live as always you've done, giving hope and joy to
others each day
So, God bless you my friend and give you His peace, whatever the
future may hold
I pray that with you He ever will stay and with comfort and love,
will enfold.

Muriel I Tate

Fortunes

People are wishing forever wishing.
Will you chance your hand on a spin of the wheel of fortune
where fate plays a hand?
That is and will be your life?
An opportunity for a change, optimism clouds my mind,
this influences my judgement to chance my hand.
For in this life of ours, who knows, hey?
Of people with their scowls and gnashing teeth
I encounter on my way on my journey.
You visit a fortune teller to influence the subconscious
to seep into the dark side,
influences along the way
but so dumbfounded are you.
Get on up, the time has come for some serious thought,
the tide is high, have you thought it through?
Think long and hard, a decision not to be considered lightly.
Before you play life's maverick card,
there'll be a few years of hardships
before you cash in your chips.
With one hesitant footstep upon life's highway,
to your destiny which has been preordained,
trust in this, it will be a revelation, you will be finally free.

Jonathan Covington

We Came, By Chance

(At Monte Cassino, 2001)

We called today, by purest chance,
To contemplate the vagaries of life,
And thought we could our day enhance,
By the mere reflection of your strife,
Spreading, among white rows, heads in hand,
Around your graves, so lovingly tended,
And felt that we might understand,
Silently applauding principles so bravely defended.

You answered the call, at God's command,
Giving your lives for freedom and right,
Dying for the cause, in a foreign land,
You fought hard - and won the good fight,
But the people who loved you, all too well,
Were left to grieve that you had gone,
Our lads, swallowed up in a private hell,
Your deeds of courage faced all alone.

We shall grieve your loss forevermore,
With a sadness in our heavy-laden hearts,
Deeply longing, for your presence, we bore,
Playing out, the weeping ones, our lonely parts,
Accepting your loss from our saddened lives,
Forever interred in a far-distant field,
Leaving behind heartbroken young wives,
Whose aching souls, their loss revealed.

We came, today, by chance, to contemplate,
Why thousands of our stoic young men,
So gloriously, yet fearfully, met their fate,
And whispered our prayers of gratitude then,
Decrying the oft said 'What fools men are,
Who go to war, their destiny to await,'
For they sought not glories from afar,
And we came, by chance
Finding Heaven's wide gate,
And prayed, for their safe haven
At last.

Julia Eva Yeardye

Thank You Lord

O Lord of sea and sky and earth,
I thank you that your lowly birth
Has made me now a child of worth
In Jesus Christ my Saviour.

O Lord of sky and earth and sea,
I thank you that your love for me
From sin and death has set me free
In Jesus Christ my Saviour.

O lord of earth and sea and sky,
I never cease to wonder why
You came to Earth in love to die
In Jesus Christ my Saviour.

So may my daily attitude
Be always one of gratitude
For Jesus Christ my Saviour.

David Varley

Life's Treasures

Glitter and gold and glamour and such
Life's treasures to hold onto that mean so much
But the mind's data bank is the most precious of all
That regurgitates the priceless when put on recall
So harvest your moments in life's tapestry store
So your winters are warm with a rich memory store.

Doris Hoole

For All To See

Let no cloud dim my reason to rejoice,
I give thanks and sing with joyful voice.

Age has slowed me, no reason to haste,
I enjoy all I do, with slower place.

Good music I listen to, old songs I sing,
I jigged once, now watch others do their thing.

Long ago, I loved to walk a country lane,
Now I enjoy views from a high windowpane.

I see God's growth of flowers amidst a velvet of green,
Trees stretching to Heaven above, to me a wonderful scene.

Over chimney pots, I watch a flock of birds in flight,
When a day is over, sometimes I see a glorious sunset at night.

All this and much more there is to see,
For all tomorrows, I'm grateful what's out there for you and me . . .

Gladys Davies

Sonnet 116

Let me not to the marriage of true minds
Admit impediments; love is not love
Which alters when it alteration finds,
Or bends with the remover to remove.
O, no, it is an ever-fixèd mark
That looks on tempests and is never shaken;
It is the star to ever wand'ring bark,
Whose worth's unknown, although his height be taken.
Love's not Time's fool, though rosy lips and cheeks,
Within his bending sickle's compass come;
Love alters not with his brief hours and weeks,
But bears it out even to the edge of doom.
If this be error and upon me proved,
I never writ, nor no man ever loved.

William Shakespeare

Freedom

I want to laugh and dance, and sing and shout.
I want to run and jump about.
I want to cry and yell, 'Yippee!'
Because today -
        Today I'm Free!

Jennifer Houghton

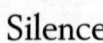

Silence

Silence can be happiness
Silence can be sad
Silence can be penetrating
Silence can be bad
Silence can cause tension
Silence can drive us mad
Silence can be wonderful
Silence can be unbearable
Silence can be just nice
If two people love silence
It is a great gift
To lighten the noise around us
And bring some peace.

Mary Guckian

I Know Not

I often wonder how life will go
Can we alter just one jot?
What is to come - we cannot know.

The river of life is in full flow.
Whatever we're given is just our lot.
I often wonder how life will go.

Have we ever been here long ago?
We cannot know whether we have or not,
What is to come - we cannot know.

The more we ask - our questions grow.
There must be some plan or some kind of plot.
I often wonder how life will go.

How will it end and where will we go?
Will Earth cool down or get searing hot?
What is to come - we cannot know.

I'm nearing the end of my journey so
I know time is the thing I haven't got.
I often wonder how life will go,
What is to come - we cannot know.

Betty M Irwin-Burton

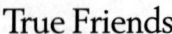

True Friends

Can you not see that we love you?
Friends who are faithful and true.
Strangers no more because you opened your heart.
A united family where we all play our part.
The caring, sharing, the loving and giving.
True friends like these
Make each day worth living.
Lift up your head then and make your choice,
Saying thank you with a clear-sounding voice.
For the world in general is much the same,
Needing a scapegoat, or someone to blame.
But true friends are worth more than gold,
A warmth and comfort out of the cold.
Your life's enriched and from now on,
Accept these friends that you have won.

Bernice Sharpe

Tomorrow

Tomorrow I will listen to the voice
that tells me to swim complete in the
level-headed lake

tomorrow I will greet with zeal
and ease all I happen to meet on the way
(but then)
tomorrow I will bask in the privacy
of my own woody remoteness

tomorrow I will walk through fields
of boundless yellow buttercups and
distinguish each one by its uniqueness

tomorrow I will appreciate and
honour the transience of a butterfly's
unparalleled life

tomorrow I will sprint to the summit
of an immeasurable mountain and there
command my freedom

tomorrow I will lie down in the long
grass and imagine your face in the clouds

tomorrow I will drink and eat but only from
the fruit bush and the unselfish stream

and tomorrow I will cheer and applaud the
flawless fanfare performed by the songbirds
at dusk.

Freddie Moorhead

Just Smile

A little goes a long way
If you just use it well.
How far a friendly smile can go
It may be hard to tell.
'Tis certain that a happy smile
Can brighten someone's day
And shorten every mile they tread
Along a dreary way.

A smile is like the sunshine
Entering all on whom it beams,
Thawing rigid, frozen hearts,
Releasing rippling streams
Of laughter, and of hopefulness,
Till stress-bound souls relax,
A smile conveys a message
Without pen or phone or fax.

If all around seems darkened
By man's fears and greeds and hates,
Mistrust between close neighbours,
Hideous wars between the states,
If faced with so much sorrow
There seems little you can do,
Go out and fill the world with smiles
Until the light breaks through.

V E Godfrey

God's Love

Through the shock and pain of death and loss,
His love shines through,
The darkest cloud that covers us,
His love shines through.

The anger, fear and loneliness,
His love shines through,
A love that guides and soothes all fear,
That wipes away each tear.

He comes to us, He comforts us,
And strengths us anew,
He holds us up and carries us,
His love shines through.

The gaping hole, the searing loss,
The change of circumstance
When all we see is darkness,
His love shines through.

When suddenly the sky is blue,
The clouds have disappeared,
Our tears are dry, a smile appears,
We owe it all to the Lord, our God.
His love shone through.

Edwina Crowley

Let Sorrow Lie In The Heart Of God

Let sorrow lie in the heart of God.
Tomorrow, we may know why,
But today, lie
In the lip-held praise
Of spring, dazed
With blue of bluebells in the hedges,
Edged with campion pink
And stitchwort white,
The cuckoo calling from the hidden hill,
Calling, calling, echoing
To break the bounds of abundance
In the heat's haze.
The day's eyes open to the stretch,
Pink-tipped of the sun's rays,
Reflecting gold at the centre
Of the day's praise.

Tomorrow we may know why.
Today is the answer.

Rosemary Wells

Our Country Park

With miles of open countryside
And little paths to roam,
For dog owners a peaceful haven
A wonderful home-from-home.
And as you go walking along,
There is often the chance of a chat
With kindred spirit dog lovers,
And the dogs too are keen on that.
They have their chances to meet,
And it's usually a friendly exchange.
We like them to have a bit of a sniff -
Enemies are soon out of range.
Are we not lucky to have such a place?
Long may it last we all say.
So property developers, one and all,
You just keep out of the way.

Joan Chapman

A Better Way

Half a laugh is better than none
Against the things which weary us,
In this world so serious
With all its troubles and woes.
Does anybody suppose,
When the angels look upon
These lives we struggle to lead,
Each longing to be freed,
Do they scratch their wings and wonder
At the ways we blindly blunder
Along a lifetime's course?
Making mistakes at every turn
Because we'll surely never learn
To appreciate the fact
This Earth on which we're tightly packed
Wishes us to pause . . .
The magic that is everywhere
If we only stopped to stare
For long enough to be reminded
Happiness is where we find it,
There it lingers.
The human race is quite absurd:
Far better if we'd all preferred
Concentrating on sheer joy
Instead of things that just annoy -
The bliss which this would bring us!

Jonathan Goodwin

If

If you can keep your head when all about you
Are losing theirs and blaming it on you;
If you can trust yourself when all men doubt you,
But make allowance for their doubting too;
If you can wait and not be tired by waiting,
Or, bring lied about, don't deal in lies,
Or, being hated, don't give way to hating,
And yet don't look too good, nor talk too wise;

If you can dream - and not make dreams your master;
If you can think - and not make thoughts your aim;
If you can meet with triumph and disaster
And treat those two impostors just the same;
If you can bear to hear the truth you've spoken
Twisted by knaves to make a trap for fools,
Or watch the things you gave your life to broken,
And stoop and build 'em up with worn-out tools;

If you can make one heap of all your winnings
And risk it on one turn of pitch-and-toss,
And lose, and start again at your beginnings
And never breath a word about your loss;
If you can force your heart and nerve and sinew
To serve your turn long after they are gone,
And so hold on when there is nothing in you
Except the Will which says to them: 'Hold on;'

If you can talk with crowds and keep your virtue,
Or walk with kings - nor lose the common touch;
If neither foes nor loving friends can hurt you;
If all men count with you, but none too much;
If you can fill the unforgiving minute
With sixty seconds' worth of distance run -
Yours is the Earth and everything that's in it,
And - which is more - you'll be a Man my son!

Armistice

The Tannoy's message, indistinct, came through the store
As thoughts of routine weekly bargains crossed my mind
And I continued with my all important task
Of bagging every small white mushroom I could find

The volume rose - a little clearer than before
But I dismissed the drift of what was being said
Until the words 'two minutes silence' made me stop -
Glance up to realise the place had gone quite dead

A sudden hush - the buzz had ceased as people stood
Upright and still, both young and old, their faces grave
And I stood with them thinking - what on earth is this
How very odd for all these shoppers to behave . . .

And then a 'thank you' rang throughout - the crowds dispersed
As all and sundry moved again, and in a while
I stopped a staff to ask precisely what I'd missed
As he advanced towards me briskly down the aisle

A lad, quite tall - just half my age and peering down
As if to say - I would have thought you'd know, my dear -
'Eleventh day! Eleventh month! Eleventh hour!
To him the data he conveyed was crystal clear

I thanked him lamely with 'of course' then made my way
Towards the paper stand where furtively I read
A day for Armistice had been reintroduced
So we could stop - reflect and honour the war dead

And every year since then eleven stakes its claim
As does the poppy much displayed with public pride
Throughout a land where gentle Autumn's ebb and flow
Recalls that consequential stemming of the tide.

Jo Lewis

Remember To Give Thanks

Remember to give thanks
For things for which you prayed
When the going was tough
And when you were afraid.

Remember to give thanks
As the one above knows best
Which way to guide in darker days
And which way will be blessed.

Remember to give thanks
When all things turn out well
More than your heart desired
And more than tongue can tell.

Still praise His name
Who heard your prayer
In time of need
And gave His care.

Patricia Fazackarley

A Well-Loved Room

I left a rose behind me,
The hour I went away,
I knew that it would wither
Before the close of day.
And yet I felt its fragrance
Would linger in the air,
And make the room feel cherished,
Although I was not there.
For every room needs loving,
If it would ever be
A haven of contentment
And deep serenity.

Lorna Wells

Angels Within

Amongst us there are angels,
No wings or halo shown.
But yet amongst us they do walk,
Never to be known.
They bring us hope and comfort,
When we need it most.
They cleanse the shadows of our mind,
Destroying ghoul or ghost.
The angels know of God,
And what he has to give.
The angels are within us all,
The reasons we should live.

Geoffrey Woodhead

Look And Listen

When we awake from our sleep
be it daylight or before dawn
let it not be in a hurry
filled with doubts or worry
let our minds and souls be rested

our thoughts pure and true
not tainted with self-doubt
our resolve solid though tested
the walls never breached
let not worry wounds fester
but fuel the heart with joy
that of the court jester

let us live life's dream
boy, girl, husband or wife
not gathering trouble and strife
for as coal is to a fire
repentance is to the soul

let this old world turn
the fields of hell burn
milk in the churn turn to butter
geese fly south for the winter
let us fly as if on eagle's wings

hear the robin sing
enjoy the first taste of spring
feel the breath of your tender lips
not listen to the words of the restless wind
for that would be a sin
show us the way, and where to begin

for, if left alone and not guided
the path isn't always clear with no map provided

Maurice Hope

So What's Good About Winter?

As dusk begins to settle, I lie still, looking out from my bedroom
window. Squirrels and birds are scampering and fluttering;
scavenging for food and lining nests. Indoors, I am warm and well fed;
cushioned from the harshness of the Wild. I lie back, listening to
some beautiful music; sipping on a warm drink. The pinkish gold of
Sunset has faded imperceptibly, into a pale Nordic blue.
Scantily clad branches of spindly trees are tossed in the breeze,
as they and I seem to sigh with one accord.

Sophie Jordanov

335

An Angel In Wellies

An angel in wellies
was playing in the sand
and when he saw me
he asked to take my hand
and together we walked
through the sands of time
laughing and talking as
if old friends
reminiscing about old times
when it appeared
as if I was there again
though I knew it could not be
yet it all seemed so real to me
and I wanted to stay
but the angel smiled and said
you can stay awhile
before you return
to those who love you and need you more.
Then he hugged me and said he must go
and as he was leaving
I asked him why he wore wellies
and he answered with a smile,
'I have to wade
through tears of grief and unhappiness
until I can restore joy.'
And when I looked again
his feet were bare

Jan Maissen

As Time Goes By

Time has a nasty habit
of simply slipping by
and the little things we meant to do
are forgotten with a sigh.
Of course they were important
and very soon we find
that yes, the things that are out of sight
very soon go out of mind -
That letter that we said we'd write,
the coffee that we'd share,
the telephone call we promised
that just vanished in thin air -
Well perhaps they didn't matter
all that much, it might be true
but it all looks slightly different
when the forgotten one is you.
In this busy world it's easy
to forget the clock ticks on
and suddenly we wonder where
the days and months have gone.
And when a conscience falls asleep
there will always be that danger
that this could be the very time
when a friend becomes a stranger.

Donald S Ferguson

Our Help

When will I call it,
Each come a day
Am ever beholding to be so, convey,
The hours spent in happening
Oft shaping one's worth,
Have come here, to help us
On place we call Earth
We've all understanding, as best that we can,
To help those but less off,
Their worries for man
May be it woman, whoever applies,
They all need our help, given
Throughout their said lives,
Others more lucky they have all of need
But should share their good luck
God so decreed
The help you give will be its worth
Will come back ten-fold,
Much richer then, you will be,
Lots more to life than gold
Help my people less well off
And rich will be reward
Have faith and help where'er you can
Give all your regard.

Hugh Campbell

Forever Near

I'd like to sit beside you
And talk to you for a while
I'd like to be near you
To see your lovely smile
I'd like to put my arms around you
And cuddle you as before
Your laughter I'd like to hear once more
A cheerless hush now fills the air
Where you sat, an empty chair
Memories linger of one I loved so dear
May love keep your spirit forever near.

Gertrude Schöen

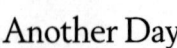

Another Day

Many a day or season has passed,
Many a year fulfilled.
The clouds their shadows will cast,
Letting the wintry snow spill.
The snow glides gently to our feet
Casting shadows of grey and white.
While in the meadow the lambs do bleat,
Huddled together out of sight.
The clouds are of a yellowy-grey,
As the earth is covered without a sound
With winter's new affray.
Snowmen, fat and round
Help children laugh joyously in their play.
Jack Frost is here this morn,
Sending forth his wintry scorn,
Covering the oaks, elms and pine.
Another day or season has passed,
Another year fulfilled.

Frederick Fordham

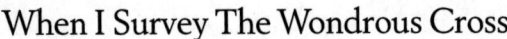

When I Survey The Wondrous Cross

When I survey the wondrous cross
where the young Prince of Glory died,
my richest gain I count but loss,
and poor contempt on all my pride.

Forbid it, Lord, that I should boast,
save in the cross of Christ, my God:
all the vain things that charm me most,
I sacrifice them to his blood.

See, from his head, his hands, his feet,
sorrow and love flow mingled down!
Did e'er such love and sorrow meet,
or thorns compose so rich a crown?

Were the whole realm of nature mine,
that were an offering far too small;
love so amazing, so divine,
demands my soul, my life, my all.

Isaac Watts, 1707

Lucky Lady

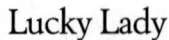

I have a little boy
And I have a little girl
I have a diamond ring
And I have a lace of pearl
I have a loving husband
And a home in which we sing
If I could wave a magic wand
I wouldn't change a thing

Carey Sellwood

Hope

When you think that no one's there,
And life is just too tough,
When everything's against you
And the future's looking rough,
Try not to give up living, though
You're close to losing hope,
For life can still surprise you
While you're clinging to that rope.

Charlotte Dudley

Just As I Am

Just as I am you take me, Lord.
You love me - o so much,
You never expect us to put on a front
To feel your tender touch.
You just want us to pray and give you our lives
So that you can work therein,
To hand you our burdens and cares of today
And be forgiven of our sin.
The love that you showed us at Calvary
Was the greatest gift of all,
And whatever we give you in return
We know will be so small.
But we try hard to do as you ask us to do
Even though it is sometimes tough,
For we know that you are with us Lord
When perhaps the going is rough.
You love and care for each one of us
And I thank you - o Lord - for that love
And know that each day, as we walk in your way,
You are guiding us all from above.

Hilary Vint

A Friend In Need

It's so hard to believe in a person
When you're feeling as low as you can,
But I know there is someone there for you
A woman, a child, or a man.
Try and let them get close up to you,
Tell them your fears and your pain,
Let them help you work through it,
To make a whole person again.

Rodney Epstein

No Charge!

This is a day I'll not forget,
I received a gift with thought.
It wished me well and was not signed
'Twas a gift that no one bought.

First gift I ever have received,
'Tis genuine, with no charge.
It has made me shed a good few tears
Because it has not left me scarred.

I learn today that someone cares
Tho' unknown my kind friend's name.
Someone understands me well
And wishes me no pain.

I raise my eyes to Heaven above.
Thanking God for such a friend.
Ask blessings for the one God knows,
The one who helps this heart to mend.
 By the grace of God.

Rosie Hues

A Helping Hand

One good deed deserves another
That's what people say
Do one good deed for someone
As we travel on our way
Help someone who's lonely
Show them that you care
Give a smile, a helping hand
Don't just stand and stare
Ease somebody's burden
This should be our creed
Don't just glance and walk away
When you find someone in need
We all need a special someone
To tell our troubles to
Don't forget, the one in need
Some day - may be you.

Lydia Barnett

Think Positive

If you feel that life has lost its sparkle,
And the light is fading from your mind,
Try to put things in perspective,
Relax, take it easy and unwind.

Don't dwell on past mistakes,
Look forward, don't look back,
Write down the pros and cons,
And make a plan of attack.

Look at all the positives,
Leave the negatives behind,
The road to recovery may be long,
But not impossible to find.

Anne Leeson

Advent - The Coming

Anguish in the cold child's eyes,
Devastation in Bethlehem's heart,
Violence in the soldier's cries,
Everywhere, conflict, greed and hate.
No hope, no joy, no heaven, now.
This is our world.

Anticipation in the shepherd's eyes,
Devotion in His mother's heart,
Veneration in the angel cries,
Eternal hope for all mankind,
New birth, new born, new heaven, now.
The Lord is here.

Anne P Munday

The Hand Of Friendship

I see the hand of friendship
Reaching out eternally
Into the lives of people
Seeking someone's empathy;
It reaches out to extricate
The sorrows that initiate
A lifetime of despondency.

The hand of friendship teaches
One another how to live
Regardless of the discord
And man's failure to forgive;
When there is animosity
The hand of friendship instantly
Defuses all things negative.

Without the hand of friendship
Showing great humanity
This life would be repressive
For mankind's majority;
And its compassion nullifies
The indiscriminate replies
From those who ply barbarity.

I see the hand of friendship
Striving endlessly to bind
The nations of this planet
As the fleeting years unwind;
For friendship will invalidate
The world's unnecessary hate
And elevate all humankind.

Iaian Wade

The Singers

God sent his Singers upon earth
With songs of sadness and of mirth,
That they might touch the hearts of men,
And bring them back to heaven again.

The first, a youth, with soul of fire,
Held in his hand a golden lyre;
Through groves he wandered, and by streams,
Playing the music of our dreams.

The second, with a bearded face,
Stood singing in the market-place,
And stirred with accents deep and loud
The hearts of all the listening crowd.

A gray old man, the third and last,
Sang in cathedrals dim and vast,
While the majestic organ rolled
Contrition from its mouths of gold.

And those who heard the Singers three
Disputed which the best might be;
For still their music seemed to start
Discordant echoes in each heart,

But the great Master said, 'I see
No best in kind, but in degree;
I gave a various gift to each,
To charm, to strength, and to teach.

These are the three great chords of might,
And he whose ear is tuned aright
Will hear no discord in the three,
But the most perfect harmony.'

Henry Wadsworth Longfellow

351

Whatever We Seek

How strange through all our lifetime
We seek an inner peace
Seems sometimes it evades all our efforts
Through the years as we try to succeed
When we are younger
There is so much to do
Our lives seem to bustle along
We are searching for newer horizons
Never knowing quite where we belong
Then as life brings the years
Things will change some
Then at last you then find what you need
For inside here at last
You have found it
That wonderful sweet inner peace

Jeanette Gaffney

Up North

It always snowed on Christmas Eve
when I was a lass up north.
With all odd socks on frozen hands,
we bravely would go forth.

We looked like sardines, all six of us
in a bed on Christmas Eve,
all listening for paper crackles,
wondering what we would receive!

A sack of coal, that's all you'll get
me mam used to shout up the stairs.
If you're not asleep in half an hour
I'll be up those apples and pears!

At 4am we'd all creep down,
skipping the stair that creaked.
We'd open the door to see if he'd been,
feeling the tension that had built up for weeks.

A selection box, a colouring book,
a compendium for all to share.
A box of crayons, a smokers set,
it's the most wonderful time of year!

Tina Aldus

Love

When a seed of love is planted
It puts out shoots round another heart.
Sometimes the shoots become tangled
And the heart is broken, till watered by tears,
New plants grow and love blossoms.
Then, when the velvet petals fall,
It mellows into autumn fruits
That keep us fed into the winter of our lives.

Joyce Walker

Life Begins At 60

Life begins at 60, by then you have more time
Life begins at 60, read about it in this rhyme
One learns to take things easy, not to rush around
Slowing down comes easy, that's what I have found
Over 60s clubs are fun and you make new friends
You will find new interests, on this a lot depends
Every day's a challenge, you don't know what it holds
Something nice can happen as the day unfolds
By the time you reach 60 you know what life's about
You know a lot about most things, that's without a doubt
One has time to think at a slower pace
Ignoring the fast life of the human race
I enjoy being 60 and I don't feel old
The only think I don't enjoy is when the weather's cold!

Brownie

In The Bleak Mid-Winter

In the bleak mid-winter
Frosty wind made moan.
Earth stood hard as iron,
Water like a stone;
Snow had fallen, snow on snow,
In the bleak mid-winter
Long ago.

Our God, heaven cannot hold Him,
Nor earth sustain;
Heaven and earth shall flee away
When he comes to reign:
In the bleak mid-winter
A stable-place sufficed
The Lord God Almighty
Jesus Christ.

Angels and Archangels
May have gathered there,
Cherubim and Seraphim
Thronged the air;
But His Mother only,
In Her maiden bliss,
Worshipped the Beloved
With a kiss.

What can I give Him,
Poor as I am?
If I were a shepherd, I would bring a lamb;
If I were a wise man,
I would do my part;
Yet what I can I give him -
Give my heart.

Christina Rosetti

Life's Highways

As we travel life's highways and byways
Experience its ups and its downs
 It's friends that we meet
 The strangers we greet
That leven our lives till it shows.

As we travel life's highways and byways
Experience its laughs and its frowns
 It's those that we know
 The friendships that grow
That helps us along every mile.

Dora Watkins

Beneath The Leaf

I was walking alone and I stepped on a leaf
So I stopped, and I thought, I wonder what's beneath?
Simply an ant passing by?
Or maybe the home of a dragonfly?
An innocent spider crawling along?
Or otherwise where did a beetle belong?
A stash of honey that belonged to a bee?
Who wouldn't be very happy with me!
A small black fly eating its dinner?
Or the resting place of a poor caterpillar?
The spot where a ladybird did casually creep?
Or the place where a snail had decided to sleep?
So I warn all those walking out there
As you are walking take time and take care.
For you may be about to step on a leaf!
Stop and think what could be beneath!
For all of the above could be just down there!
And it takes only one footstep to destroy and not care.
I hope you understand the lives of these small creatures
And remember not to demolish some of Earth's great features.

Lily Rose White (12)

Open Your Eyes

Open up your eyes to see
How beautiful this Earth can be
The birds and animals, this Earth so old
The plants and flowers, trees so bold
The sights and sounds, smells and colours
All the people we know are our sisters and brothers
Why do we treat this Earth so bad
Taken for granted, so very sad
But the earth will forgive if given some time
If you're thoughtful, willing and kind
So please open up your eyes to see
This Earth so beautiful, is there for you and me

Elizabeth Hall

Sorrow Is A Blackness

Sorrow is a blackness
Deep and dark and blue
No one can touch inside
No one can see or do

It is a long, hard journey
Just to get through
Passing days just fly past
The weeks just go too

One day you smile a little
Perhaps have a laugh
It's a shock to hear yourself
Such a long time has passed

A dear friend has helped you
Each and every day
You haven't even noticed
Beside you all the way

Turn around and start again
A new dawn is here
Goodbye tears and sadness
Time to reappear

Life is not easy
No one said it was
Friends and loved ones are close by
Why? Maybe just because

Carol Sheppard

Following The Snail!

Following the silver trail of a purple striped snail,
my miniaturised body entered insectworld.
I jumped on top of giant puffballs, skated
along shimmering trails of slimy slugs,
ate giant bags of candyfloss-like pollen,
rode the bumper beetles, rested awhile.

Met Mr Millipede and Mrs Maggot.
Had lunch at their famous bistro,
consisting of dead human hair,
flakes of skin, broiled toenails,
and strawberry snot for afters!

Jumped from the top of daffodils,
into soft silken spider webs.
Tripped the light fantastic,
played by the 'grating grasshoppers',
as glow-worms flashed in sequence,
around the cavernous disco floor.

Won three stuffed humans,
got soaked on the spitting newt ride.
Went upside down on the spinning ladybird
and tomorrow . . .
I'm going to the bottom of the garden,
with my magnifying glass, again.

Danny Coleman

361

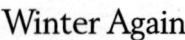

Winter Again

The hills and dales
Are all covered in snow
Flakes falling gently
Float like a billion stars
Over the trees and meadows
Footprints in the snow
For all to see
Children slide down
The hills on sledges
Snowman stand regally
Carrots for noses
A joy to behold
Log fires crackling
Roast chestnuts popping
Slippers by the hearth
It's winter again.

P A Kirby

Résumé

I don't know how long has gone by
since your offer of sunshine
transforming me and this life of mine,
loosening-knitting all there is
into a new pattern of unimaginable unity.
You have written your signs
wherever I turn my eyes;
the vertical trees in the changes of light,
the majestic mountains capped with snow,
the waterfalls splashing on the golden rocks,
the flight of birds in the variable sky,
the placid cows in the flowering fields.
You have written your signs within me.
There is nothing within and without
which is mine.
Your eternal yes,
echoed by a choir,
is signing all time and space
and it will be forever sunshine
on your resurrection.

Angela Matheson

They Could Save Us Yet

Is the sturdy teddy bear
The last defence against machinery?
See the loathesome pylons march
Across the once-glad verdant scenery.
They represent old-fashioned ways;
They're laptops with built-in affection,
For you can trust a teddy bear
To guide you in the right direction.
They're just the thing when you feel blue
And all your world is in a muddle;
And all they need, these bears so true
Is just a really super cuddle.

Leo Taylor

364

From This Day Forward

A saying we don't hear much of now
The only time you hear it is taking a vow
Most of the vows are taken in court
To sort out the carnage that someone has wrought
Why is the world consumed with greed?
Most people have all they need
Yet there is no peace in the world today
Because most people are walking away
And ignoring the time when we answer to our maker
Be it sooner or later.

Mary Tickle

Dawn Chorus

You get up in the morning
A bright new day
But how do you greet
This brand new day
When you don't feel
Up to a greeting so gay
You hobble around
In another world
Hoping soon
To be out by this twirl
Then enough is enough
A visitor calls
Your hair hasn't seen the comb
Oh no! That's the phone
Can't come round
On my day off
I'll make some coffee
And some toast
Try to be the hostess
Well almost
Then at last
When left alone
Little me will pledge
To look like something
Not dragged through a hedge.

Margaret Parnell

366

The Glow Of Christmas

The days have quickly passed
Some of which one wished to last
But they come and go
As everyone doth know
Life going forward
As a river doth flow onward

With autumn leaves long gone
One bursts into song
With Christmas in view
Folk buying something new
Presents to be bought
Using precious time to sought

After all the rushing
And overcoming the bustling
Folk wrapped in silence
Reminiscing their experience
With feelings just fine
Preparing for Christmas time

A happy time of the year
With loved ones near
Folk filled with anxieties
Preparing for festivities
But graciously carrying on
Trusting nothing will go wrong

Children excited with their antics
The young feeling romantic
Old and young join in
Looking with a frown or grin
Folk going to mass
'Tis the 'glow of Christmas'

Josephine Foreman

367

December 19th

Life's What You Make It!

You're born into a world full of people, full of expectations,
hopes, fears and dreams.
You have a whole life ahead of you.
Many years to do all that your heart desires.
What you do, and whether you achieve it . . . is up to you!

Some people see to live, others live to see.
Some people hear to live, others live to hear.
Some people taste to live, others live to taste.
Some people touch to live, while others live to touch, or be touched.

Some people speak to live, others live to speak.
Some people eat to live, others live to eat.
Some people sleep to live, others live to sleep, and dream.
Some people move to live, while others can only dream to move.

Some people live to work, others work to live.
Some people live to earn, others earn to live.
Some people live to lead, others lead to live.
Some people shop to live, while others shop like tomorrow
was their final day.

Some people travel to live, others live to travel.
Some people kill to survive, others live to kill.
Some people love to live, while others spend forever waiting to live,
to love, or be loved.

Some people want to live, others live to want!
Some people live to die, while some die while wanting to live!

Life's what you make it!
You only have one!
Do everything that you want to do, don't waste any time . . .

The world is yours, make the most of it,
And remember, *nothing is impossible if you follow your heart!*

Lynsey Tocker

368

A Helping Hand

A helping hand is what is needed
On our pathway through life
To make each day a little brighter
To resolve troubles and strife

Someone who understands our needs
Or who can find another way
To lighten up our darkness
Who answers when we pray

The helping hand may be a child
Who brings you sheer delight
To watch all his antics
As he holds the limelight

The helping hand is an angel
Who offers you insight
We all walk with angels
Who help to spread the light

The angel is a messenger
In any shape or size
Whose heart is guaranteed to warm
With words that are so wise

If you've problems you just cannot solve
Or if you're feeling blue
Just reach out to another soul
And he will help you through

So never think that you're alone
With no-one who will care
Just reach out to your fellow man
You'll find us everywhere!

brightlaurastar

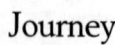

Journey

Life begins at the beginning of life,
With a cry,
A sigh,
One smile of delight.

Then into the night, life sleeps, deep.
Not knowing where pathways lead -
 or futures go, but stretch the hand
                              of the unknown.
But, encompassing tide, drifts and dies.
To bring out the best in all we are.
To leave no scar on life.
Love, yes love all you know and care,
Protect,
And then let go.
Be the one, that we must be,
From cradle,
Youth,
Towards eternity.

T Lawrence

Achievement

To have 'achieved' gives an inner glow
Of satisfaction. Well done you!
It raises self-esteem, fills one with pride
For a success that cannot be denied.

There are great achievers among men
And women, all of renown'd fame
In Literature, Science and the Arts
World travellers exploring foreign parts.

The mole that tunnels through the soil
The huge hill made by the ants' toil
The birds that yearly build their nests
These are achievers at their best.

Some are helped on their way to reach
The top. But nevertheless they achieve.
But those that make it on their own
That is the jewel in their crown.

Lisa Wolfe

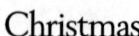

Christmas

Cold and frosty the winter looms,
And we close ourselves into our cosy rooms.
Snow transforms the neighbourhood,
We may not welcome it, but it does look good.
Christmas trees with their colourful lights,
Stars shine brightly on a frosty night.
Everything is a wondrous sight,
Carol singers with their sweet rendering.
The children wondering what Santa will bring,
On the radio it's White Christmas from Bing.
Children play out in the snow,
From the window mums watch them as they put on a show.
Dads are rushing to finish that toy,
The cot's for the girl, the train's for the boy.
And for the baby a cuddly toy,
Made by granny with such loving care
As she sits in her comfy old chair.
Mum's in the kitchen finishing off the cake,
The children are put to bed but they're still awake.
They're all excited, it's Christmas Eve,
They're wondering what Santa will leave.
At last the children are all asleep,
Into the bedrooms mum and dad both creep,
To lay their presents beside each bed,
Dad with his outfit all white and red.
They plant a kiss on each child's head.
They put out the light and close the door,
They go downstairs and a sherry they pour,
They've done their best, they can do no more.
On TV there's a Christmas show,
Outside everything's covered with snow.
Inside from the fire there's a nice, warm glow,
Soon to bed they'll be on their way,
Tomorrow they'll celebrate Christmas day.

Irene V Haywood

'Twas The Night Before Christmas

'Twas the night before Christmas, when all
through the house
Not a creature was stirring, not even a mouse;
The stockings were hung by the chimney with care,
In hopes that St Nicholas soon would be there;

The children were nestled all snug in their beds,
While visions of sugar-plums danced in their heads;
And mamma in her 'kerchief, and I in my cap,
Had just settled down for a long winter's nap,

When out on the lawn there arose such a clatter,
I sprang from the bed to see what was the matter.
Away to the window I flew like a flash,
Tore open the shutters and threw up the slash.

The moon on the breast of the new-fallen snow
Gave the lustre to mid-day to objects below,
When, what to my wondering eyes should appear,
But a miniature sleigh, and eight tiny reindeer,

With a little old driver, so lively and quick,
I knew in a moment it must be St Nick.
More rapid than eagles his coursers they came,
And he whistled, and shouted, and called them
by name;

'Now, *Dasher!* now, *Dancer!* now, *Prancer* and *Vixen!*
On, *Comet!* on *Cupid!* on, *Donder* and *Blitzen!*
To the top of the porch! to the top of the wall!
Now dash away! dash away! dash away all!'

As dry leaves that before the wild hurricane fly,
When they meet with an obstacle, mount to
the sky,
So up to the house-top the coursers they flew,
With the sleigh full of toys, and St Nicholas too.

And then, in a twinkling, I heard on the roof
The prancing and pawing of each little hoof.
As I drew in my hand, and was turning around,
Down the chimney St Nicholas came with a bound.

He was dressed all in fur, from his
head to his foot,
And his clothes were all tarnished with
ashes and soot;
A bundle of toys he had flung on his back,
And he looked like a peddler just opening his pack.

His eyes - how they twinked! his dimples how merry!
His cheeks were like roses, his nose like a cherry!
His droll like mouth was drawn up like a bow,
And the beard of his chin was as white as the snow;

The stump of a pipe he held tight in his teeth,
And the smoke it encircled his head like a wreath;
He had a broad face and a little round belly,
That shook, when he laughed like a bowlful of jelly.

He was chubby and plump, a right jolly old elf,
And I laughed when I saw him, in spite of myself;
A wink of his eye and a twist of his head,
Soon gave me to know I had nothing to dread;

He spoke not a word, but went straight to his work,
And filled all the stockings; then turned with a jerk,
And laying his finger aside of his nose,
And giving a nod, up the chimney he rose;

He sprang to his sleigh, to his team gave a whistle,
And away they all flew like the down of a thistle.
But I heard him exclaim, ere he
drove out of sight,
'Happy Christmas to all, and to all a goodnight!'

Major Henry Livingstone Jr
(Previously believed to have been written by
Clement Clarke Moore)

Things Unusual

It was a most unusual night,
The sky with myriad stars alight,
One shone more brightly than the day
Above a shed where cattle lay.

To this an unusual couple ran:
A teenage girl, an older man;
A cry in the night, a searing pain,
And on the hay a babe was lain.

It was a most unusual birth:
The Eternal God come down to Earth,
Maker of all that one could name,
Confined within a human frame.

He was a most unusual King:
Of earthly riches, not a thing;
No throne with ivory surround,
Sharp, piercing thorns his only crown.

Unusual gifts with him he brought:
Inner healing for all who sought,
Love and forgiveness, peace and grace,
And in his heart, a hiding place.

The centuries, this message spans,
So come to Him with open hands;
'Twould be a most unusual thing
To spurn a present from a King!

Catherine O'Connor

The Groom

I want to touch him all the time
I want to be with him every hour
I want to walk beside him in the snow
I want to shelter with him from a shower

I want to kiss his warm, soft lips
I want to lie in his arms tonight
I want to wake up with him beside me
I want to love him always with all my might

I want to share with him my dreams
I want to have children with this man
I want to whisper sweet nothings and to grow old
With you, the man soon to become my husband

Mary Allen

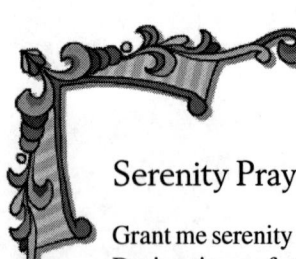

Serenity Prayer

Grant me serenity Lord, I pray,
During times of stress and strife,
To accept the things I cannot change
And get on with my daily life.

Grant me courage Lord, I pray,
To change the things I can,
That there be no needless suffering
For myself or fellow man.

Grant me wisdom Lord, I pray,
That I may clearly see,
Things to accept or things to change,
Lord, my guide and mentor be.

Serenity, courage, wisdom,
I daily seek from Thee,
That I may live a life that's free
From fear and anxiety.

Years Long Ago

We may have been poor to other folks,
but we had fun all the same.
Pa made us toys from pieces of wood,
while Ma knitted clothes for rag dolls.
Our tiny cottage was always warm,
as turf was neatly stacked.
Fresh scones or flap-jacks stood
waiting for hungry mouths to fill.
While at night on cold winter nights,
showers blew the hawthorn bush.
Pa played his fiddle, as Ma sang like a lark,
so pretty she sang.
My brother and I had tears in our eyes
as her voice rose into the air.
Above lay the loft where my sisters all four
huddled under thick eiderdowns.
Outside a fox stirred the chickens,
that clucked out of control,
squawking and flapping their wings,
as the fox crept nearer.
Pa fired a shot from his gun,
but alas the fox escaped once again.
It brings a tear to my old grey eyes,
as I glance at the old photos I hold,
but memories of years long ago
will remain in my heart, I know.

Maureen Connolly

A Kingfisher

Its colour is there for all to see,
As it flits across the river with its great colours,
Dipping, here and there, as it sights a fish,
Its flash of turquoise, is no other.

With bright eyes, watching and waiting,
It suddenly darts across the floor,
Catching its prize within the fresh water,
It takes to a branch, with its great slither.

Rosemary E Pearson

Just Look

The brightness of snow is dazzling, glittering all around,
When the snug blanket of winter is cushioning the ground,
The sun makes radiant colours, thro' diamonds in a ray,
It feels good to be living, when nothing stands in the way.
Forgotten a beautiful morning when darkness takes its grip,
How could something so wonderful really turn to this.
Yet darkness has its values, if only we could find,
Balance of God's natural truth, if we don't store fear in the mind.
So wake up amongst the confusion, mankind has thrown in our way
And remember the morning sunshine, that comes simply to say,
'Do not be afraid' 365 times in The Good Book,
A light shining thro' the dark, when we care to look.

M Burleigh

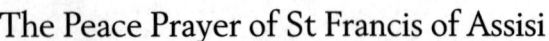

The Peace Prayer of St Francis of Assisi

Lord, make me an instrument of your peace,
Where there is hatred, let me sow love,
Where there is injury, pardon,
Where there is doubt, faith,
Where there is despair, hope,
Where there is darkness, light.
and where there is sadness, joy.

Grant that I may not seek so much
To be consoled, as to console,
To be understood, as to understand,
To be loved, as to love.
For it is in giving that we receive.
It is pardoning that we are pardoned.
And it is in dying, that we are born to eternal life.